TABLE OF CONTENTS

THE PARSON AND JACK RUSSELL TERRIERS

Sheila Webster Boneham, Ph.D.

Interpet Publishing

The Parson and Jack Russell Terriers

Project Team
Editor: Stephanie Fornino
Copy Editor: Joann Woy
Design: Tilly Grassa
Series Design: Mada Design
Series Originator: Dominique De Vito

United Kingdom Editorial Team
Hannah Turner
Nicola Parker
Claire Cullinan

First published in the United Kingdom in 2007 by
Interpet Publishing
Vincent Lane
Dorking
Surrey
RH4 3YX

ISBN 13 978-1-84286-143-1

Printed and bound in Indonesia.

This book has been published with the intent to provide accurate and authoritative information in regard to the subject matter within. While every precaution has been taken in preparation of this book, the author and publisher expressly disclaim responsibility for any errors, omissions, or adverse effects arising from the use or application of the information contained herein. The techniques and suggestions are used at the reader's discretion and are not to be considered a substitute for veterinary care. If you suspect a medical problem consult your vet.

INTERPET
PUBLISHING

www.interpet.co.uk

HISTORY

of the Parson and Jack Russell Terriers

Over the past decade, a certain type of lively little terrier has become better known to the general public than ever before in the century and a half he's been around. In fact, the bright, intelligent face and attractive small size of these lively little terriers win them many admirers, but all too many people forget the real dog that lies within. Like all breeds, the Parson Russell Terrier (PRT) and Jack Russell Terrier (JRT) we know today were developed for a specific purpose. The traits that made their ancestors successful in pursuit of that purpose remain with today's Parson and Jack Russell Terriers, making them perfect companions for some people and four-legged nightmares for others.

The breeds known today as the Parson Russell Terrier and the Jack Russell Terrier originated in England in the nineteenth century, when Parson John (Jack) Russell bred a small terrier designed to bolt small game, particularly fox, from their lairs. As we shall see, two similar but distinct types of terriers eventually developed in England from the Parson's original dogs. Although differences exist between modern Parson Russells and Jack Russells, their personalities and physical traits still reflect their fox-hunting heritage.

Parson Russell and Jack Russell Terriers are small, compact, and flexible, enabling them to enter and manoeuvre in the close quarters of an underground den. Their predominantly white coat makes them highly visible. In addition, they have the energy and stamina to follow hounds and horses for miles across hilly terrain, and the intelligence, courage, and tenacity to find and face their quarry. Their intelligence, size, and good looks attract attention, and in the right environment, Parson and Jack Russell Terriers are fine companions.

Prospective owners must understand, though, that their heritage as a working terrier means that these dogs are not couch potatoes, and they have minds of their own. It will be easier to understand the characteristics of the modern Parson Russell and Jack Russell, which will be discussed in more detail in Chapter 2, if you have some knowledge of the breeds' histories and original purpose.

THE PARSON/JACK RUSSELL TERRIER IN ENGLAND

The history of the Parson Russell and Jack Russell Terrier is thoroughly entwined with the landscape and rural society of the southern part of the breed's native land, and with one man's passion for foxhunting with hounds, horses, and of course, terriers, so let's begin our journey in England.

Parson Russell and His Terriers

The Parson and Jack Russell Terriers take their names from Parson John (Jack) Russell, who bred some of the finest terriers used for foxhunting in Devonshire, England, in the mid to late 1800s. Russell preferred a terrier who was bold enough to follow a fox "to earth"—into its den—and yet restrained enough to bolt (flush) it for the foxhounds and mounted hunters rather than kill it.

Russell, who was born in 1795, became interested in fox terriers at an early age. When he was 16 years old, he and another student secretly kept a pack of four and a half couples (nine terriers) at their boarding school. Hiding that many boisterous dogs must have been quite a feat, and the miscreants were eventually discovered by school authorities. Russell's partner in crime was expelled, and Russell himself thrashed. Undeterred in his pursuit of knowledge, Russell went on to earn his bachelor's and master's degrees at Oxford. His passion for foxhunting also continued to burn bright, and he rode when he could with the Beaufort, Bicester, and Old

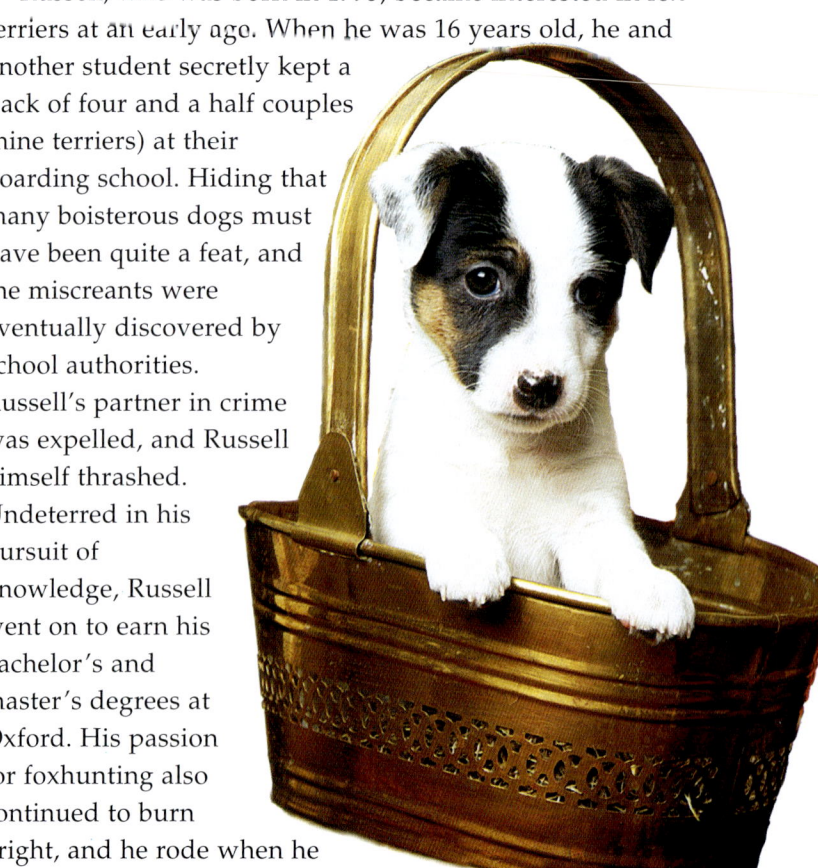

Berkshire hunt clubs. He was ordained in 1820 and returned to Devon as a curate, assisting the parish priest and hunting when he could. In 1826, Russell married another avid foxhunter, Penelope Bury. He spent his career at various parishes throughout Devonshire and continued to hunt on the moors and to breed fine terriers until he died on April 28, 1883.

In southern England, where Russell lived, foxhunting was a mounted sport over open fields. Terriers who hunted fox in that environment needed to be leggy enough to keep up with hounds and horses, and they were expected to "bolt" their quarry, or drive it from its den. That's the type of dog Parson Russell bred. For breeding and hunting, Russell and other enthusiasts selected terriers of very uniform size: 14 inches tall (35.6 cm), weighing 16 to 18 pounds (7.3 to 8.2 g), with chests measuring 14 to 16 inches (35.6 to 40.7 cm) in circumference—about the size of a red fox.

Parson Russell's terriers were predominantly white, with tan or black-and-tan markings.

Russell's terriers were distinctive for being predominantly white, with tan or black-and-tan markings limited to the head and base of the tail. He also insisted that his dogs be "steady from riot," meaning that they should not be overcome by bloodlust and kill the quarry. Russell's terriers bayed from underground if the fox wouldn't bolt, letting the "terrier man" who trained and handled them dig into the den and free the fox so that the mounted pursuit could continue. Dogs who tried to kill the fox underground were often said to have the more aggressive bull terrier in their ancestry, so brindle colouring—typical of bull terriers—became a disqualification in the Parson and Jack Russell breed standards.

Russell was a founding member of the Kennel Club, established in England in 1873. He was also known as the "Father of the Wire-haired Fox Terrier," and his terriers' bloodlines contributed to both sides of the pedigree of the well-known bitch called L'il Foiler, whose son was the influential Wire-haired Fox Terrier champion, Carlisle Tack. Russell's dogs also featured in the pedigrees of many Smooth Fox Terriers, to whom he bred to improve the coats of his own broken-coated terriers.

Changes in farming practices altered the nature of foxhunting in southern England in the late nineteenth century, and the cost of hunting on horseback became prohibitive for all but the very wealthy. Terrier sport changed, too, as the dogs ceased to follow hounds and horses and were instead carried to fox and badger dens and released to go underground to kill their quarry or pull them out. All sorts of working terriers were lumped together as "Jack Russell Terriers," but many lacked the intelligence, stable temperament, and physical traits—length of leg, short back, and drop ears—prized by Russell and his cohorts. Many of the dogs imported to North America and presented to the public as Jack Russell Terriers have been typical of these "pretenders," with short legs, long backs, prick ears, and frequently stubborn and aggressive personalities. Clearly, a breed standard was needed to define the breed.

Russell Terriers are small, compact, and flexible.

Standardising the Parson Jack Russell Terrier

Fortunately, some terrier fanciers in southern England continued to breed terriers of the type favoured by Russell, and in 1904, Arthur Heinemann, a well-known terrier man and founder of the Devon and Somerset Badger Club, drafted the first breed standard for the Parson Jack Russell Terrier, a 12- (30.5 cm) to 14-inch (35.6 cm) terrier with the physical and mental traits of the breed's early dogs. Heinemann founded the Parson Jack Russell Terrier Club in 1914, and its members kept the breed alive.

A breed standard for the Parson Jack Russell Terrier was finally drafted in 1904 to distinguish him from other terriers.

In the early 1970s, the height limit for the dog was expanded from the original 12 (30.5 cm) to 14 inches (35.6 cm) to a more inclusive 10 (25.4 cm) to 15 inches (38.1 cm). The problem many people had with the wider range of sizes, though, is evident at both extremes, and proponents of the narrower height limits hold that a 10-inch (25.4 cm) terrier is too small to perform the original function of Parson Russell's terriers—bolting a fox from its underground lair. A 15-inch (38.1 cm) dog, on the other hand, is too large to go into an underground fox den and turn around. The standard was eventually changed again in 1984 to state that the ideal height for a dog (male) is 14 inches (35.6 cm) and for a bitch (female), 13 inches (33.0 cm). In September 2002, the Kennel Club recommended that "lower" heights be considered "acceptable provided that soundness and balance are maintained," and the standard now specifies 13 (33.0 cm) to 14 inches (35.6 cm) as ideal but allows that "smaller terriers are required for work in certain areas and lower heights are therefore

Eddie the Television Star

The part of Eddie, the Jack Russell Terrier on the popular American TV show Frasier, was played by a multitalented dog named Moose and Moose's stunt-double and real-life son, Enzo. Moose, who was born in Florida along with his nine littermates, also played the part of Skip in the big-screen release of My Dog Skip. (Enzo played the young Skip.) You can read more about this versatile JRT in My Life as a Dog, penned by Moose with some help from his co-author, Brian Hargrove.

quite acceptable provided that soundness and balance are maintained."

Thanks to the efforts of the Parson Jack Russell Terrier Club, the Kennel Club recognised the Parson Jack Russell Terrier as a breed effective January, 1990, making him eligible to show in Britain. In 1999, the Kennel Club voted to change the name of the breed to Parson Russell Terrier, and the club in turn became the Parson Russell Terrier Club.

One of the original functions of Parson Russell's terriers was to bolt a fox from its underground lair.

Memorable Dogs

Parson Russell founded his breeding programme on a dog named Trump, whom he bought from a local milkman in 1819, while still a student at Oxford. Trump was a white fox-sized terrier with patches of dark tan over each eye and ear, and a small spot of tan at the base of his tail. He had a weather-resistant coat of close, thick, slightly wiry hair, straight legs and tight feet, and an athletic build that reflected his stamina and strength.

Jack Russells

For more information on the Jack Russell Terrier Club of Great Britain, visit its website at www.jackrussellgb.co.uk

The three fox-hunting terrier breeds—the Smooth Fox, Wire-haired Fox, and Parson Russell—were developed by breeding selectively for different traits, but all have a number of ancestors in common. One strain of Smooth Fox Terriers traces back to a bitch named Juddy, whose dam was Russell's bitch, Vic. Juddy also figured prominently in the development of the Parson Russell Terrier; Juddy had a daughter named Moss I in 1869, and she in turn produced a daughter named Moss II. Moss II was bred to Tipp II, a dog bred by Russell, and produced a bitch named Wasp, whom Russell sold to fellow terrier fancier Thomas Wooten. In 1883, Wasp was bred to Young Foiler, who was also descended from Juddy, and produced a bitch named Li'l Foiler. In 1884, she was bred to a dog named Trick to produce Carlisle Tack. As we saw earlier in this chapter, Carlisle Tack was influential in the development of the Wire-haired Fox Terrier, but he also sired a dog named Carlisle Tyro, who had the traits of a modern Parson Russell Terrier and was important to the further development of the breed.

Despite their common ancestry, though, three distinct types of white fox-hunting terriers had emerged by the last decade of the nineteenth century. The type that came to be called the Fox Terrier could be found in two forms: the smooth-coated and the wire-

Timeline in England

- 1904: Arthur Heinemann drafts first breed standard for the Parson Jack Russell Terrier.
- 1970s: Height limit for Parson Jack Russell Terrier expanded from the original 12 (30.5 cm) to 14 inches (35.6 cm) to a more inclusive 10 (25.4 cm) to 15 inches (38.1 cm).
- 1984: Standard changed to state that the ideal height for a dog (male) is 14 inches (35.6 cm) and for a bitch (female), 13 inches (33.0 cm).
- 1990: The Kennel Club recognises the Parson Jack Russell Terrier as a breed.
- 1999: The Kennel Club votes to change name of the breed to Parson Russell Terrier, and the breed club consequently becomes the Parson Russell Terrier Club.
- 2002: The Kennel Club recommends that lower heights be considered acceptable, and the standard is changed to specify that a height of 13 (33.0 cm) to 14 inches (35.6 cm) is ideal, although smaller terriers are also acceptable if they prove sound and balanced.

Parson and Jack Russell Terriers were known in the US at least as early as the 1930s.

haired. Cross-breeding between the two eventually stopped, and the two types diverged as entirely different breeds—the Smooth Fox Terrier and the Wire-haired Fox Terrier. The third fox-hunting terrier was the older type once owned and bred by Russell and others who favoured his specific qualities. These became known as the Parson Jack Russell, Jack Russell, or Parson Russell Terrier.

The term "Russell" came to be used in common parlance to mean just about any cross-bred hunting terrier. To some extent, the misuse of the name was accidental, just as people commonly use brand names to refer to whole classes of products. But the fine reputation of the Parson's dogs was also exploited for profit. Annie Harris, who was related to Russell's one-time kennel man, Will Rawle, was one of many people who found that she could easily sell the cross-bred terriers she produced if she called them "Jack Russell Terriers." Unfortunately, many of the dogs presented today around the world as Parson Russell Terriers or Jack Russell Terriers are of mixed ancestry and do not exhibit the traits outlined in the breed standards. They may be perfectly nice dogs, but Parson or Jack Russell Terriers they are not.

THE TERRIERS IN NORTH AMERICA

Although Parson and Jack Russell Terriers were known in the United States at least as early as the 1930s, it was not until 1976 that enthusiasts banded together to form the Jack Russell Terrier Club of America (JRTCA). The primary goal of the JRTCA was and still is to preserve the working abilities of the Jack Russell Terrier. Its members believe that affiliation with multi-breed organisations will work against their primary goal, with detrimental effects on the

breed, and they therefore strongly oppose registration or affiliation with the AKC, UKC, and other such organisations.

Some breeders and fanciers, however, felt differently, and in 1985, a group of them got together and formed the Jack Russell Terrier Breeders Association (JRTBA) in order to, as the association puts it, respond "to widespread misrepresentation in America of the Jack Russell Terrier as a long-backed, short-legged, heavy-bodied terrier of questionable temperament, measuring 10 (25.4 cm) to 12 inches (30.5 cm) and incapable of following a fox anywhere." The goal of the ten original members was to "help restore and breed to the original Parson Jack Russell Terrier breed standard," and to that end, the association based its breed standard on the original standard written by Arthur Heinemann in 1904. The standard defines the Jack Russell Terrier as a working breed designed specifically to hunt the red fox by tracking the fox above ground and following him underground to

Breed Club Info

For more information on the various breed clubs governing Parson Russell Terriers and Jack Russell Terriers, you can visit a few websites.

You can visit the Kennel Club site at www.the-kennel-club.org.uk, which will give contact details of the Parson Russell Terrier Breed Club.

All enthusiasts of this fine breed are interested in preserving his working abilities.

AKC Status

In 1996, the Jack Russell Terrier became the 145th breed registered by the American Kennel Club. Effective April 1, 2003, the name of the breed was changed to Parson Russell Terrier, and during that year 1,554 Parson Russell Terriers were registered with the AKC, putting the breed at number 61 out of 151 AKC breeds in popularity.

Different attitudes and rules apply to the long-legged and short-legged terriers in the various organisations that recognise them.

bolt him for the hunter. Among other things, the standard specifies a height range of "12 (30.5 cm) to 14 inches (35.6 cm) to eliminate the short-legged terriers."

Beginning in 1987, the JRTBA began working toward American Kennel Club (AKC) recognition for the Jack Russell Terrier. In 1992, and again in 1996, the club revised the breed standard according to AKC guidelines regarding structure and layout, and in 1996, the standard was declared acceptable by the AKC.

On April 23, 1997, JRTBA members voted to change the name of the association to the more inclusive Jack Russell Terrier Association of America (JRTAA). The goals and purpose of the association remained the same, but membership and activities were no longer focused only on breeders. In July of 1997, the AKC Board of Directors unanimously accepted the Jack Russell Terrier into the AKC registry, effective November 1, 1997. The JRTAA later requested that the name of the breed be changed, and effective April 1, 2003, the name Parson Russell Terrier became the official AKC name for the breed. The JRTAA subsequently became the Parson Russell Terrier Association of America (PRTAA).

The United Kennel Club (UKC) recognises long-legged Jack Russell Terriers in two sizes: 10 (25.4 cm) to 12½ (31.8 cm) inches and over 12½ (31.8 cm) inches to 15 inches (38.1 cm). They also recognise the short-legged Russell Terrier, who stands 10 (25.4 cm) to 12 (30.5 cm) inches high.

THE PARSON AND JACK RUSSELL AROUND THE WORLD

Different attitudes and rules apply to the long- and short-legged terriers in the various organisations that recognise them. The FCI (Fédération Cynologique Internationale, or World Canine Organisation), which governs shows in many countries outside North America, recognises the Parson/Jack Russell Terrier as originating in England and uses the British breed standard, which specifies a height of 13 (33.0 cm) to 14 inches (35.6 cm). The FCI also recognises the Jack Russell Terrier as a separate breed originating in Australia and accepts the Australian standard, which specifies a height of 10 (25.4 cm) to 12 inches (30.5 cm). The Australian National Kennel Council (ANKC) and the Irish Kennel Club (IKC) make the same distinction.

By whatever name they go, the modern terriers descended from Parson Russell's working dogs share many distinguishing traits, particularly a big attitude in a compact, tough little body. That bold, intelligent, die-hard attitude is undoubtedly what has kept these terriers popular through more than a century, despite the politics and varying preferences of the people who love them.

The CKC and CPRTA

The Canadian Kennel Club (CKC) does not recognise the Parson or Jack Russell Terrier, but the Canadian Parson Russell Terrier Association (CPRTA) offers registration, breed information, and competition for Parson and Jack Russell Terriers. The CPRTA uses the British breed standard.

Timeline in the United States

- 1976: Enthusiasts form Jack Russell Terrier Club of America (JRTCA).
- 1985: Group of breeders and fanciers break away from the JRTCA and form the Jack Russell Terrier Breeders Association (JRTBA).
- 1996: JRTBA's breed standard is accepted by the AKC.
- 1997: JRTBA members vote to change the name of their association to the more inclusive Jack Russell Terrier Association of America (JRTAA). In same year, AKC Board of Directors unanimously accept the Jack Russell Terrier into the AKC registry.
- 2003: JRTAA request that name of breed be changed to Parson Russell Terrier granted. JRTAA subsequently becomes the Parson Russell Terrier Association of America (PRTAA).

Chapter

2

CHARACTERISTICS

of the Parson and Jack Russell Terriers

Parson and Jack Russell Terriers, like all breeds of dogs, are easily identified by certain physical and behavioural traits related to the purpose for which each breed was developed. Over many generations, breeders chose individuals who were able to perform a specific function or set of functions, and those physical and mental characteristics eventually became set and highly predictable in well-bred animals. But why does the original purpose of the breed matter to you? After all, you probably don't plan to hunt fox, and the furriest prey your dog is likely to chase is a tennis ball. But whether or not he has the opportunity to use his hunting instincts, every Parson or Jack Russell Terrier has them to some degree, and they affect his behaviour, for better or for worse, if he's your pet. It's important to understand the traits that make these terriers what they are, because although a Parson or Jack Russell will likely be a determined hunting dog and may work well in other sports for someone with the skills and desire to channel his intelligence and energy, he isn't everyone's ideal pet.

FORM AND FUNCTION

A saying exists among dog breeders that "form follows function." This means that the physical traits that make each breed recognisable are the result of careful breeding practices among devoted breeders who select those aspects of physical form that help the dogs perform their assigned functions. It takes many generations of selective breeding to establish a breed, as well as continuing attention to careful selection to maintain the traits and talents for which it was developed.

A document called a *breed standard* is eventually developed by devotees of a breed to define the physical, mental, and behavioural characteristics they seek in their dogs. The breed standard also identifies traits that are acceptable but not desirable and traits that are considered detrimental to the breed, and which therefore disqualify a dog from competition in conformation shows and for breeding.

Parson Russell Terrier breed standards have been established by the Kennel Club (KC) in England, the American Kennel Club (AKC) in the United States, and other registries.

Selective Breeding

Selective breeding is the practice of carefully choosing a male and female to mate in order to reproduce desirable characteristics and to reduce or eliminate undesirable characteristics in their offspring.

Standards for the Jack Russell Terrier have been established by the Jack Russell Terrier Club of America (JRTCA), the Jack Russell Terrier Club of Great Britain (JRTCGB), and other organisations. In this chapter, we'll see how the KC breed standard for the Parson Russell Terrier, and the Jack Russell Terrier Club of Great Britain breed standards for the Jack Russell Terrier, define the ideal member of each breed. (You will find the complete standards for both breeds in the Appendix.)

The Parson Russell Terrier Breed Standard

The KC standard introduces the Parson as essentially a working terrier. Dogs must have the ability and conformation to go to ground and run with hounds. For this reason, Parsons have a workmanlike appearance. They should be active and agile, and built for speed and endurance. The overall picture should be one of balance and flexibility.

A Parson must also have the right temperament and attitude, and should be bold and friendly in all his dealings. The KC standard states that honourable scars are permissible.

Size

Physically, the Parson Russell Terrier is small. Make no mistake, though—this is still a lot of dog to live with and handle! The KC standard states that a working terrier should be capable of being spanned behind the shoulders by average-sized hands. The ideal height for a dog (male) is 14 inches (35.6 cm), and for a bitch (female), 13 inches (33.0 cm).

Individuals, of course, vary in height, and a Parson Russell who is slightly over or under the ideal height but otherwise conforms to the breed standard won't be penalised for size in the show ring. The KC breed standard has been revised in order to state that it is recognised that smaller terriers are required to work in certain areas, and lower heights are acceptable provided that soundness and balance are maintained.

The ACK standard states that PRTs over 15 inches (38.1 cm) or under 12 inches (30.5 cm) are disqualified from competing in conformation classes, and most responsible breeders will not use dogs who are too small or large in a breeding programme. A PRT in proper working condition normally weighs between 13 pounds (5.9 kg) and 17 pounds (7.7 kg).

Head and Skull

The PRT's head should look strong and should be in proportion to the body. The top of the skull should be flat, fairly broad between the ears, and gradually narrowing to the eyes. The stop—the spot between the eyes where the back of the head meets the muzzle—should be shallow. In other words, you should be able to see clearly where the forehead ends and the muzzle begins, but there shouldn't be a sharp angle at that spot. The length of the muzzle from the end of the nose to the stop should be slightly shorter than the length of the skull from the stop to the occiput, the pointed ridge of bone at the back of the skull. The nose must be completely filled in with black pigment; a liver (brown) nose is faulted.

The term "terrier" comes from the Latin "terre," or "ground." All terriers are "go-to-ground dogs" who are bred to follow their quarry into dens below the surface of the earth.

Jaws and Teeth

The upper and lower jaws should be solid and appear to be capable of exerting punishing strength on the dog's quarry. The teeth should be large and strong, and the dog should have "complete dentition"—that is, no genetically missing teeth. The upper and lower jaws should meet "in a perfect scissor bite" in which the upper incisors, or front teeth, fit closely just in front of the lower incisors when the mouth is closed, and the rest of the teeth are aligned straight and square to the jaws. This scissor bite

PRT and JRT Breed Differences

Parson Russell Terrier
- 13 to 14 inches (33.0 to 35.6 cm) tall
- smooth or broken coat
- registered by the KC (with representation by the JRTAA, CPRTA, and AKC)

Jack Russell Terrier
- 10 to 15 inches (25.4 to 38.1 cm) tall
- smooth, broken, or rough coat
- registered by the JRTCA, JRTCBG, and UKC

enhances the strength and stability of the dog's jaws, which are essential in a working terrier. The KC standard states that a dog will be disqualified from the show ring if four or more teeth are missing or if the bite is overshot (top teeth extend beyond lower teeth), undershot (lower teeth extend beyond upper teeth), or wry (the upper and lower jaws are not aligned lengthwise).

Eyes

The Parson Russell's eyes should be almond shaped, not round, and should be dark in colour, preferably with dark rims. They should be moderate in size and should be deep-set. The Parson Russell should look directly at you with an expression of unmistakable intelligence and eagerness.

Ears

The Parson Russell breed standard calls for the terriers' eyes to be almond shaped and full of intelligence.

The PRT should have button ears—that is, small, v-shaped ears that fold forward at or just above the skull, covering the opening of the ear and pointing toward the eyes. They should be moderately thick, not fleshy or longer than the corner of the eye. The AKC disqualifies dogs with prick, or standing, ears from the show ring.

Neck and Topline

The neck of the Parson Russell should be clean and muscular. It should be relatively long and should be moderately arched at the top rather than straight or ewe-necked. The neck should widen gradually toward the shoulders so that it blends smoothly into the body. The topline—the line of the top of the back from the high point of the shoulders (withers) to the hips—should be strong, straight, and level (horizontal to the ground) when the dog is moving. The loin, or the area directly behind the rib cage, should be slightly arched.

Body

The Parson Russell Terrier's body should appear balanced, with neither the front end nor the rear seeming larger or more powerful than the other end. The dog's back is supposed to be neither short nor long and should look strong but flexible laterally (side to side), so that the dog could turn around if necessary in an underground den or tunnel. The PRT's body should appear "square," and the height-to-length ratio can be measured in two ways. One way is to look at the dog's height at the withers (the high point at the top of the shoulder blades, behind the neck) and his overall length from chest to base of tail, which should be approximately equal. The other is to measure the dog's height at the withers and his length of back from the withers to the base of his tail. The ratio of these height-to-back measurements should be approximately 6:5.

The tuck-up is what one might think of as the belly, the underside of the body right behind the ribs. In the Parson Russell, the tuck-up should be moderate, meaning the belly should rise slightly behind the ribs. The Parson Russell's chest should be narrow and moderately deep from front to back so that the dog appears athletic, not heavy chested. When Parson Russells are shown, the judge spans the chest with her hands. The standard requires that the chest behind the shoulders must be easily spanned by average-size hands, such that the thumbs should meet at the spine and the fingers under the chest.

A breed standard identifies the physical, mental, and behavioural characteristics that people seek in their dogs.

Ribs

The ribs are not over-sprung, meaning that they curve outward from the spine to allow room for the heart, lungs, and other organs, but they are oval rather than round when viewed from the front or rear of the dog. The lower edge of the ribs should not be lower than the dog's elbows; if they are, the elbows will be forced out, interfering with efficient movement.

Tail

The Parson Russell Terrier's tail is set high and carried gaily, or straight up in the air. In the US, PRT tails are customarily docked so that the tip of the tail is about level with the top of the skull. That much length was to allow a hunter to get a good grip on the tail if necessary to pull or lift the dog.

Gait

The breed standard describes the PRT's movement as being free-striding. It should be well-co-ordinated with straight action front and behind. This allows the dog to move well and do his job with maximum efficiency and minimal risk of fatigue or injury. The Parson Russell should appear lively, well coordinated, and unrestricted when in motion, and should have a long, straight stride at a trot. The essential components of functional forequarters and hindquarters are strong, well-formed bones; proper angles where the long bones come together; joints that allow for free, clean movement; and compact, round feet with thick, tough pads and moderately arched toes that point straight ahead.

Coat

Parson Russell Terriers should reflect a balanced image.

Parson Russells come in two types of coats. Both are double coats, meaning that a short, dense undercoat lies close to the skin and protects it from cold, brush, and other outdoor hazards. The undercoat is covered by an outer or top coat. In the smooth PRT, the outer coat is made of coarse, dense hair that lies flat to the body. The broken coat is coarse and straight and lies close to the body, but it is slightly longer above the eyes and under the chin, giving a hint of eyebrows and beard. Hair covers the entire dog, including the belly and undersides of the thighs. Soft, silky, curly, or woolly coats or lack of undercoat are considered incorrect. Parson Russells are not supposed to be groomed excessively when they are shown.

Colour

The Parson Russell Terrier may be white, white with black or tan markings, or tri-colour, a combination of white, black, and tan. Black and tan markings on the body are not desirable—these colours are preferred on the head and the base of the tail only. The colours should be strong and clear, although grizzle (white hairs mixed into the colour) is acceptable.

Adherence to the breed standard is essential for the potential show dog.

The Jack Russell Terrier Breed Standard

The Jack Russell Terrier Club of Great Britain was established in 1974 to promote the working terrier. It has its own breed standard and holds a national show, but it is not recognised by the Kennel Club, which has adopted the Parson Russell Terrier as its 'official' breed. Many parts of the breed standard for the Jack Russell Terrier describe, understandably, essentially the same characteristics as do the equivalent parts of the KC standard for the Parson Russell Terrier. There are a few differences in content and emphasis, though. The Jack Russell standard begins by emphasising that the dog's attitude, disposition, and physical traits should reflect his status as a working terrier. Jack Russells may stand between 10 (25.4 cm) to 15 (38.1 cm) inches tall, giving them a wider range of sizes than the Parson Russell. Descriptions of the two breeds' heads are very similar, asking for V-shaped ears and dark, almond-shaped eyes. The body size and shape are also similar with the same requirement that the chest should be easily spanned by average-sized hands.

A Balanced Body

"Balance" refers to the physical proportions that enable the correctly constructed dog to perform his job, particularly the appearance and relative proportions of the parts of the head, head-to-body, and height-to-length. "Balance" is also used to refer to equality of the angles of the joints between the long bones in the front and hind legs.

Three coat types are permissible in Jack Russells—smooth, rough, and broken. Both breeds are to be predominantly white, and the standard states that brindle markings are unacceptable.

In the show ring, old scars and injuries do not penalise a terrier's chances unless they interfere with its movements, or with its utility for work or stud. For judging, terriers are classified into two groups: 10 to 12.5 inches (25.4 to 26 cms) and 12.5 to 15 inches (26 to 38 cms).

DO RUSSELL TERRIERS MAKE GOOD PETS?

Parson and Jack Russell Terriers should have a confident and alert appearance.

If you're contemplating adding a Parson or Jack Russell Terrier to your family, you must remember that his forebears were bred to work long days following foxhounds and horses over hill and dale, and then to enter the fox's den, face a frightened carnivore, and chase him out. To work well and happily in such conditions, a dog needs to have nearly inexhaustible energy, a high pain threshold, courage, determination, and the ability to solve problems on his own. People who understand and properly manage these traits with exercise, training, and a sense of humour enjoy life with an outstanding canine companion dog. But when people misunderstand or mismanage the same traits, they end up with a dog they don't want in their lives. Most of the Parson and Jack Russell Terriers found in rescue programmes and centres are there simply because they behave like typical specimens of their breeds.

Temperament

Most of the terrier breeds are known for certain temperament traits that equip the dogs mentally to do the jobs for which they were developed. Although the intended quarry is different for each breed, all terriers were developed to hunt other animals and chase them into their dens. A dog who enters close quarters and takes on a cornered animal that is fighting for its life must possess a certain mindset, and this is reflected in the descriptions of most terriers. Even if their relatives haven't hunted in many generations, terriers are feisty, independent, determined, clever, intense, lively, stubborn, and brave. They have a high prey drive that makes them quick to chase anything that moves, and they tend to bark. The Parson or Jack Russell is all this and more, and most of them are much closer to their hunting roots than many modern terriers. If you are considering a Parson or Jack Russell as a pet, you must take the breed's terrier instincts into account if you want a happy relationship with your dog.

The terrier's high tolerance for pain or discomfort, coupled with his feistiness and tendency to defend himself, can make him a challenge to manage. He may not even notice a tug that would stop a more sensitive dog in his tracks, and he may resent or ignore corrections that other dogs respond to easily. His high intelligence and excellent problem-solving ability make him adept at sports, tricks, and other productive pursuits when he's guided by a competent trainer, but left undirected, he may become an escape artist, landscape redesigner, and general ripper-upper of his owner's possessions. His strong prey drive can make him a hazard to other animals, and his dominant personality and tendency to respond defensively to perceived threats can make him a hazard to people who don't understand him.

Russells have boundless energy, a lot of courage, and the ability to solve problems on their own.

When working, the Russell is a keen hunter, alert to the movements of potential prey. He's tenacious, determined, and brave. As a companion at home, he's affectionate and playful. He's also a bundle of energy and quite independent. His lack of fear can get him into serious trouble, and he will chase moving targets and dig when he has a chance. If he's not kept busy, he'll find his own fun—barking, digging, and tearing things up—and he'll be far more amused by his cleverness than you or your neighbours will be. He may get a case of wanderlust and take off in search of adventure, which is not a healthy pursuit for dogs in our society.

A properly socialised and well-trained Parson or Jack Russell Terrier is a terrific dog for an active person with a sense of humour, dog training experience, and a high tolerance for canine mischief. But it's important to remember that small size and cute appearance don't make the dog—temperament and behaviour do.

Behavioural and Personality Traits

The typical Jack or Parson Russell's fundamentally terrier temperament makes for a number of behaviours that some people don't like or that don't fit well in certain environments. In fact, most Russells who lose their homes and end up in rescue situations are perfectly normal terriers. Their "problem behaviours" are problematic only because the dogs were in the wrong environment. Let's look at some behaviours that Parson and Jack Russell Terrier owners should expect and be willing to tolerate.

Barking

Like most terriers, Russells are quick to bark whenever they see or hear something they don't think should be where it is. Some individuals have a very high-pitched yippy bark that makes the racket downright painful for unwilling listeners. If you have close neighbours, a very vocal terrier could easily cause problems for both of you, especially if you need to be gone for long periods during the day or night and can't control the racket. Even if you aren't bothered by barking, you should never leave your terrier

Terriers are generally feisty, independent, determined, clever, and stubborn.

outside unsupervised. At worst, he may annoy someone enough to bring legal action against you, or in extreme cases, to do something to your dog. Even if your neighbours take no action, a constantly barking dog is an extreme nuisance and not a very flattering reflection on his owner.

Climbing and Digging

Another behaviour that commonly gets Russells into trouble is their ability to escape from fenced enclosures. They can easily jump a fence five times their own height. Many also climb, and they can scale fences and kennel walls with ease. And of course, they are terriers—they dig and can get under fences in no time. Many terriers also learn to open gates. To confine a terrier safely, you may need to sink fence wire under the ground around the perimeter to prevent digging, and you may need a higher fence than you think with a barrier at the top to thwart the would-be adventurer. A locked gate is also a good idea.

Chasing

The Parson or Jack Russell Terrier is not a dog you should trust off-lead except in a safely confined area. The high prey drive that makes him such an excellent hunter can lead him into trouble in the wrong environment. He will chase anything that moves—squirrels, cats, other dogs, and sometimes joggers, bicycles, or children—and he'll ignore your frantic attempts to call him back. This behaviour can be simply annoying if it takes you an hour to catch up with him, or it can be devastating if he runs into the path of a car, picks a fight with the wrong dog, nips someone, or becomes lost. For his own good, and yours, your terrier must be on lead or safely confined at all times.

Terriers enjoy digging and can easily burrow under fences and other enclosures.

Aggression

The Parson Russell Terrier should not show overt aggression towards another dog or human. However, some terriers are aggressive toward other animals, including their own kind. The Russell puppy must be carefully and thoroughly socialised if he's to get along with other dogs, and even then, many experienced terrier breeders and owners say that a Parson or Jack Russell Terrier should never be left alone with other animals, because he may attack and even kill another dog for possession of a toy or bed. Two or more terriers may also work together as a pack to kill or injure a larger dog.

Because of his strong instinctive prey drive, a Russell is likely to respond to any running animal by chasing and attacking it. He is quite capable or killing or seriously injuring other pets, including cats, rabbits, and smaller creatures. Many Russells do live in multi-pet homes, but it's absolutely essential that you understand the power of instinct and your own responsibility to prevent your terrier from hurting your own or someone else's pets. The Russells' hunting instinct doesn't make them bad dogs, but someone must be responsible for keeping their urges within acceptable bounds.

Family Suitability

If your dog's job will be simply to be a family dog, a Parson or Jack Russell is not your best choice, especially a puppy or young adult. The Russell's desire to chase and hunt simply don't fit into most household environments, and trying to suppress these instincts is usually frustrating for dog and person alike, and fruitless to boot. On the other hand, if you can keep your dog busy with activities that channel his hunting instincts and energy into appropriate alternatives, and if you can accept his typically terrier behaviours, then he may be right for you and you for him.

Parson or Jack Russells can and do perform well in competitive obedience. They enjoy and excel in agility, as well as in flyball, where their athletic abilities and prey drive can be used to negotiate obstacles and pursue flying objects. In the US, terriers can take part in tracking, which puts a dog's fine nose to work and expends energy as you follow scent trails together. Earthdog and similar activities (available in the US) are tailor-made for a Parson or Jack Russell Terrier.

Keep your terrier busy with activities that channel his energy into appropriate outlets.

Boredom is the root of a lot of misbehaviour among terriers. If you don't give your dog appropriate outlets for his instinctive behaviours, he'll find his own. He may chase cars, bicycles, joggers, and kids; guard his turf, food, toys, and family from all comers; hunt birds, wild animals, bugs, cats, and other dogs; dig, dig, dig; and bark, bark, bark. These behaviours can be a nuisance at best and dangerous at worst, but they are nevertheless natural responses to the Russell's heritage as, above all, a hunting terrier.

The truth is that, regardless of how cute he is, the Parson or Jack Russell Terrier is not the right dog for an inexperienced dog owner or one who cannot direct his behaviour effectively. To live successfully with a terrier, you need to be even more determined than your dog, or your dog will soon be in charge.

The best person for a Russell is someone who has successfully owned a terrier or another strong-willed, dominant breed, and who has developed effective training skills. In the right situation, the Parson or Jack Russell can excel as a companion and as a hunter or competitor, but he's definitely not a good match for everyone.

Terriers and Children

Movies like *My Dog Skip* portray the Jack Russell as the ideal canine buddy for children. And in certain situations and with the right children, a Parson or Jack Russell can be a great pet and a teacher of valuable lessons about love, friendship, and responsibility. But please don't bring a dog into your home if your child is the only one who wants one. No matter how a child pleads and promises to care for the dog, the fact is that an adult will be responsible for most of the dog's care. If that adult didn't want the dog to begin with and resents the extra work of caring for him, adding a dog to the household is not a good idea. The whole family should be involved in deciding to get a dog, and if anyone in the household doesn't want one, it's a good idea to resolve that issue before adding a four-footed family member.

Terriers can live happily with children if responsible adults are on hand to supervise their interaction.

Having a family dog creates a wonderful opportunity to teach children to be careful and thoughtful when making decisions that affect other living beings, but it's unrealistic and unfair to both child and dog to expect a child to assume complete responsibility for your dog. Kids' interests change over time, but your dog still needs everything he needed before, including someone's time and love. You can't toss him into a cupboard like an old toy, so before you bring him home, be sure he'll have what he needs for his whole life.

Assuming that you can commit to the dog for his whole life, you have to decide whether a Parson or Jack Russell Terrier is the right dog for your children. Lots of Russells do live successfully with kids, but you need to consider carefully the traits that make them a poor choice for some families. As we've seen, terriers have a

Basic Training

Basic obedience training is important for all dogs, but for one who lives with children it's critical, and the training should be kept up after the class ends.

strong instinct to defend themselves against actions they perceive as threatening. A child, especially a young one, may not intend the dog any harm, but the dog may not understand that. Even a well-socialised Russell may not tolerate being poked or prodded, having his ears pulled, or being teased. He will see the child either as a threat or as a "puppy" and a nuisance, and he will respond in what he thinks is an appropriate manner—he'll growl, snap, or bite to defend himself or make the child behave. Many Russells are also extremely possessive and will guard their food, beds, toys, favourite chair, spot on the sofa, and even whole rooms. Unfortunately, children are not equipped with the genes that teach puppies to recognise canine warnings and submit or back off, and the clash between the two species can be tragic for both.

Terriers can certainly live happily with children, but only if responsible adults take the time to train both the dog and the kids and supervise all interaction between these smaller creatures, especially when either is young. Your children should be taught how to interact safely and respectfully with your dog. No one—especially a child—should roughhouse or play tug-of-war or other games that encourage your terrier to grab for things or compete with people of any age for control of "resources," like food, toys, beds, and furniture. Although your dog should be taught not to guard things from people, your children also need to learn not to take things away from the dog and not to tease or hurt him. Some people seem to think that a "good" dog will take anything a kid dishes out. That's not only unfair to the dog, it's a dangerous attitude. All interaction between children and puppies should be closely supervised by a responsible adult who is in a position to intervene immediately. In addition, you can greatly reduce the risk that your dog will bite by having the dog neutered.

Trainability

The Parson or Jack Russell Terrier is intelligent and opinionated, and he has a mind of his own. He can certainly be trained, though, and many Russells do well in agility and even obedience competition. The trick is to teach him from young puppyhood on that he doesn't make the rules and that his person is the one in charge. Remember, this is a dog who has to be tough, determined, and brave to do the job for which he was designed: facing down well-armed and equally determined wild animals. The attitude that makes the terrier good at

Rules for Dog–Child Interaction

Make your child—or someone else's child—safer by teaching these basic rules for interacting with dogs.

- Never run up to a dog—walk slowly.
- Don't scream or yell around dogs.
- If you see a dog you want to pet, ask the owner first. If the owner says no, don't try to touch the dog. If the owner says yes, then walk up to the dog calmly and quietly, and let the dog sniff your open hand before you try to pet him.
- Never reach over a dog's head or touch him from behind until after he has a chance to sniff you; you may startle him, and he may snap. The best place to pet a dog is under his chin or on his chest.
- If a dog tries to get away from you, don't chase him. If you scare him, he might bite.
- If you see a dog without a person, leave the dog alone.
- Don't tease dogs. Teasing is mean and may frighten the dog or make him angry. Don't yell at dogs, and never, ever pretend to bark or growl at them.
- Never try to take food, toys, bones, or anything else away from a dog. If your dog has something he shouldn't have, ask an adult to help.
- Don't bother a dog who is eating, sleeping, relieving himself, or taking care of puppies.
- Don't stare at a dog's eyes, especially if the dog doesn't know you.
- Don't run away from a dog. If you're running and a dog chases you, stop, stand still, and be quiet. If the dog comes close to you, "be a tree"—cross your arms with your hands on your shoulders. Don't look at the dog.
- If a dog barks, growls, or shows you his teeth, look away from the dog's face and walk very slowly sideways until the dog relaxes or you're out of sight.
- If a dog attacks you, "be a ball"—get down on your knees, and curl up with your face tucked into your legs and your arms around your head. Lie still—don't move or scream.
- If a dog bites you, tell an adult right away. If you don't know the dog, try to remember where you were when he bit you, what he looked like, where the dog lives if you know, which way he went after he bit you, and who else saw him bite you.
- If you see dogs fighting, don't try to stop them! Stay away from the dogs, and find an adult to help.
- If you see a sick or injured dog, don't touch him. Find an adult to help.

his job can also make him a challenge to train. He can be stubborn, and many Russells are dominant—they believe they should rule. To train a terrier and to live with him in peace, you must teach him to respect you and every member of your household.

Teaching respect does not mean that you should manhandle or hit your dog. On the contrary, there's no reason to hurt any dog in the name of training. Physical punishments are unnecessary, ineffective, and unfair, and the Russell, like most terriers, may react defensively to physical corrections. Again, this behaviour is directly linked to the terrier's original purpose; if his prey fights back and hurts him, the Russell doesn't give up or give in. He becomes even more fierce and determined. In a training environment, if you hurt

Parson and Jack Russell Terriers are best suited to a life where they can get a great deal of outdoor exercise.

or threaten your terrier, he's likely to growl, snap, and possibly bite. If you can meet the challenges of training a terrier with a sense of humour and respect for the dog's heritage, using modern motivational training methods, you'll build a relationship of trust and get much farther, much faster.

Exercise Requirements

A tired dog is a good dog. Because of his heritage and status today as a working terrier above all else, the Russell has plenty of energy and a clever mind that's always looking for things to do. If you don't give your Russell enough physical and mental exercise, he'll find things to do on his own, and you probably won't like the results. If you want a pleasant and peaceable life with your terrier, you must see that he gets plenty of exercise and mental activity. Luckily, Russells are versatile, and it's easy to find activities that engage their interest if you put in a little time and effort. If you give him a good daily game of tennis ball retrieve, a nice long walk, and a short training session, your terrier will be more likely to settle down when you're through for the evening.

If you have the time, money, and inclination, you may want to try some of the organised sports in which Parson and Jack Russells excel—agility, flyball, obedience, earthdog, racing, and heelwork to music are all good activities for a terrier. People enjoy them, too! (See Chapter 7 for more on these and other activities.)

The Best Environment for a Parson or Jack Russell Terrier

The Parson Jack Russell Terrier came to be in the fox-hunting country of England, where he worked and played outdoors all day. As a working terrier at heart, he is especially suited to life in the country.

In the end, though, the best environment for a Russell isn't so much a location as a lifestyle. He needs an owner who will see to it that he gets the physical and mental stimulation he needs to channel his boundless enthusiasm. Can a Russell live happily in an apartment? Possibly, if his person takes him for long, long walks, trains him in basic obedience and in some other activity to challenge his mind, and finds safe outlets for him to use up energy. Can he live happily with a walk around the block and long hours confined indoors? Probably not. And if your terrier isn't happy, chances are you won't be happy, either. Terriers tend to be very active indoors as well as out, and all that energy has to go somewhere. If you don't direct it, your dog will!

On the other hand, a Russell who lives in the country without training, control, and lots of interaction with his people will be likely to wander or get into serious trouble during his undirected adventures. He needs a safe place to play, as well as supervision. The world holds many hazards for a fearless little dog, including cars, other animals, and more. It's up to you to keep him safe, no matter where you live.

If you consider carefully how a Parson or Jack Russell's inherited traits will affect his behaviour as your long-time companion animal, your chances for a successful dog-and-owner relationship will be much better. If you learn to manage his energy and instincts through training, exercise, companionship, and mutual respect, you and your terrier will be amply rewarded with a rich and loving relationship.

Many Parson and Jack Russells can be trained to excel at various sports and activities.

C h a p t e r

3

PREPARING

for Your Parson or Jack Russell Terrier

You've considered the advantages and drawbacks and have decided you're a Parson or Jack Russell Terrier kind of person. Now that the big decision is out of the way, you have to make specific choices that will lead you to the right individual dog. And before he comes home, you need to stock up on the things that will make his homecoming easier for both of you. So let's get busy!

PRELIMINARY DECISIONS

Puppy or Adult?

What could be cuter or sweeter or funnier than a little puppy? Not much, which is why most people don't think about how much work is required to raise a puppy well. A puppy will require lots of your time. He'll need plenty of exercise every single day, as well as constant supervision when he's not confined to keep him out of trouble. Even the easiest puppy to housetrain will probably pee on your carpet a time or two, and he'll most likely chew a few things when you're not watching him. He'll be a baby puppy only a few short weeks, and then he'll become an adolescent—think "teenager." He'll question your authority, ignore commands he learned and followed as a younger pup, and generally behave like, well, an adolescent. He'll need ongoing training and activities to challenge his body and mind. This period can last two years or even longer.

Nature and nurture work together to transform your puppy into an adult. Although raising a puppy lets you influence his development to some extent (for bad as well as for good) because you control his socialisation, training, nutrition, exercise, and other influences, your puppy's genetic makeup also affects the dog he will become. If you're dedicated to proper puppy training and rearing, realise that it won't all be fun, have a good mentor to guide you through the rough spots, and have a sense of humour, a puppy may be the right choice. If you don't have the time and energy to guide your young dog's development, you might be happier with an adult.

If you choose an adult terrier, what you see is pretty much what you get. If he's been neglected, you can expect him to improve with better food, care, and training, but the essential dog is already there. Are you worried that an adult dog won't bond to you? Never fear! We humans cling to the image of the faithful dog, true unto death, but outside of books and movies, most dogs are perfectly happy to love the one they're with if they get the care and attention they need. It's humbling to know we're so easily replaced, but isn't it good to know that if something were to happen to you, your dog could still live a happy doggy life?

Male or Female?

A lot of people think that females (properly called *bitches*) are gentle, sweet, and motherly and therefore make better pets than males (or *dogs*), who are supposedly scrappy, independent, and prone to wander. The truth is that hormonal cycles can make intact

(unspayed) bitches moody, distracted, and aggressive—not unlike some intact males.

The strongest influence on your dog's personality and behaviour, other than genes and upbringing, is your dog's reproductive status. The hormones related to sexual behaviour exert tremendous influence, and sexually intact terriers of both sexes are more likely than their neutered brethren to wander, bite, mark with urine indoors and out, and indulge in other annoying behaviours. If you want a steady, affectionate, devoted pet, look for a male or female terrier with a sound temperament, socialise and train him or her properly, and have him or her neutered.

When to Bring Your Puppy Home

There's a widespread belief that a puppy must arrive in his new home at exactly 7 weeks of age or he'll never bond to his new family. Not true! The "7-week myth" is based on a misinterpretation of research that demonstrated that puppies need to have positive contact with people—any people—by the seventh week. If they don't, they'll have trouble bonding to people throughout their lives. It is critical that a pup meet lots of friendly people and animals during the short time from the seventh to twelfth weeks of his life if he's to develop proper social skills, but the people he meets don't have to be the ones with whom he'll spend his life.

A puppy is ready for a new home when he is eight weeks of age or older.

Puppies go through several developmental periods, including fear imprint periods. Anything that frightens or hurts the puppy during these fear periods may remain frightening to him throughout his life, so it's important to shelter him from bad experiences at this time. The first fear period typically occurs at about 8 weeks and is often the most influential, so some breeders keep their pups until they are through this critical time.

If you're buying a puppy, ask the seller how the puppies are handled. Each puppy should spend one-on-one time every day with at least one person and begin toilet training no later than the seventh week. Even a puppy as young as 7 or 8 weeks can begin learning to sit, lie down, stand, and come on command, and start to walk nicely on a lead. He won't be able to do everything perfectly for a few weeks, but if you start teaching him simple things while he's very young, he will not only begin to learn specific behaviours, but he will learn how to learn, a skill that will last him his whole life. If you want a well-adjusted adult Russell, do not get one who hasn't been handled between the seventh and twelfth weeks, and don't take one home at this age if you can't spend lots of time with him.

BREEDERS

Puppies are hard to resist, but don't fall for a poorly bred puppy. It's definitely to your advantage to take the time to find a responsible breeder who is committed to the health and well-being of her own dogs and the breed. Such a breeder works hard to breed physically and mentally healthy animals, to make each generation better than the one before, and to give her puppies a good start. She matches dams and sires carefully, provides good prenatal and postnatal care, and closely monitors her puppies and bitches before, during, and after the birth. She socialises her puppies and will try to pick the right puppy for you.

Sometimes breeders have adult terriers available who make perfectly nice pets.

If you've decided you'd prefer not to tackle puppy raising but your dog's history and breeding are important to you, you might find a nice older puppy or adult terrier available from a breeder. These may be pups who haven't lived up to their early promise for competition or breeding, or retired show or breeding dogs who would be happier with one-on-one attention, or grown-up puppies returned to the breeders due to divorce, illness, or other reasons.

How to Find a Responsible Breeder

Most responsible breeders don't advertise in the newspaper, so you'll have to use other sources to find one. Start with the Parson Russell Terrier Club and the Jack Russell Terrier Club of Great Britain. In most cases, the secretary will maintain directories of breeders. You can find out about breeders on the KC website at www.the-kennel-club.org.uk. If you see a dog you like, talk to the owner and find out who bred the dog. Attend a dog show, and purchase a catalogue—it lists the names of the dogs and their breeders and the names and

addresses of their owners, so even if you can't talk to them at the show, you can call or e-mail them later.

Why should you look for breeders whose dogs are competing if you just want a nice pet? The reason is that most responsible breeders participate in activities that test their dogs' instincts, abilities, and quality. A good breeder tries to produce her next great dog in every litter, but not every puppy will have what it takes to be competitive. Most puppies, in fact, are destined to be pets—a fine destiny for a dog! The factors that keep those puppies out of competition may be so minor that you might not see them even if the breeder shows you.

Occasionally, you can find a good breeder and well-bred puppy through a newspaper or magazine advertisement, but most of the advertisments you see, especially in newspapers, are placed by pet breeders, who will not have bothered with a well-researched breeding programme. Be careful, too, about ads in dog magazines; it is all too easy to be swayed by an attractive advert, which may be placed by an unscrupulous breeder. You'll be investing time, money, and emotions in the dog you bring into your life, and the more carefully you choose your pup's breeder, the happier you'll all be in the end. A responsible breeder:

- keeps her puppies until they're at least 7 weeks old;
- welcomes questions and answers them willingly;
- asks you lots of questions;
- wants you to visit and meet her dogs;
- belongs to one or more dog clubs;
- screens all her breeding dogs for inherited diseases;
- knows the inherited problems that occur in the breed and does not claim that her dogs' bloodlines are free of health problems (there's no such thing as a "clean line");
- requires you to neuter your pet puppy;
- tells you about the challenges of owning a terrier;
- handles and socialises her puppies;
- keeps her dogs in a clean environment;
- knows every adult dog and every puppy as an individual;
- willingly refers you to her previous buyers;
- asks for and checks your references;
- does not charge extra for "papers";
- does not pressure you to buy a puppy; in fact, she makes you prove you're good enough to own one!

Visiting Breeders

Don't visit two breeders in a row, because it's very easy to carry diseases and parasites from one place to another on your skin, clothes, and shoes, even if everything looks clean. To prevent the spread of diseases and parasites, shower and change into clean clothes and shoes between visits.

Dog breeding done responsibly is not a business in the usual sense. When you call a breeder, you're calling her home, not a shop or factory. She probably has several dogs and a human family, a job, and other interests and obligations. Call at a reasonable hour, and offer to call back if it's not a good time for her. Don't expect a breeder who doesn't know you to return long-distance calls at her expense. Many breeders have websites that you can locate with a search engine and which may answer a lot of your questions. Many breeders also prefer initial contacts by e-mail, so that they can answer when it's convenient.

When you call or write, ask questions and be prepared to answer some. Breeders sometimes speak "doglish," so if you don't understand something, ask for clarification. Trust your instincts. You should be entering a long-term relationship with this person, so if you're uncomfortable, thank her for her time and move to the next breeder on your list.

A well-informed novice breeder is much better than someone with years of irresponsible breeding behind her, but experience does have value. If the person is new to breeding Parson or Jack Russell Terriers, you'll have to decide whether her answers to your questions make you confident that she knows the breed. Ask why she bred this bitch to this dog, and ask about the strengths and weaknesses of the individuals and their bloodlines. Even if you don't know a lot about Parson or Jack Russell pedigrees, you'll be able to tell whether the breeder seems to know about the puppies' ancestors. Serious breeders can recite pedigrees from memory, and they know a lot about the traits, good and bad, that various ancestors are likely to pass along. Beware of anyone who breeds more than two or three different breeds or who has bounced frequently and repeatedly from one breed to another.

The breeder's facilities should be clean and in good repair.

Signs of a Healthy Puppy

A healthy 7- to 12-week-old puppy:
- is solid and well-proportioned;
- is well covered with flesh and doesn't have a potbelly;
- has soft, shiny fur;
- has healthy skin with no red or bald spots, and no fleas;
- has a clean anal area;
- has bright, clear eyes;
- has pink gums and healthy, slightly musky "puppy breath;"
- has properly aligned jaws and a correct bite;
- has a clean, slightly damp nose with no sign of discharge;
- breathes easily without sneezing, coughing, or wheezing;
- has clean ears;
- moves well with no signs of lameness or other problems;
- is happy and playful—except when he's asleep!

The breeder should show you registration papers, health clearances, title certificates, pedigrees, and other paperwork related to the litter. If she doesn't offer, ask to see documents supporting any claims she makes about the dogs. Don't buy from any breeder who can't show the paperwork or who resents your request or says you can see the paperwork after you buy the puppy. That would be like a car dealer telling you the age and make of a car after you pay for it.

The puppy's dam (mother) should be available for you to meet. She may not look her best after caring for puppies for several weeks, but a well-cared-for dam will not look exhausted, malnourished, or ill. She may be protective of her puppies, but she should accept you when the breeder vouches for you, and she should be reasonably friendly when away from the puppies. The sire (father) may or may not be present. If he is, you should meet him, too. If not, the breeder should be able to show you pictures of him and copies of his health clearances, title certificates, pedigree, and registration. If other relatives of the litter are there for you to see, this is even better. If you don't like the puppy's parents, grandparents, and other relatives, don't buy the puppy.

The breeder's facilities, whether in her home or a kennel, should be clean and in good repair. The dogs should look healthy and well cared for. They should have room to move around and play, and they should have access to fresh water. There should be an obvious bond between breeder and dogs, and the breeder should be able to tell you about each puppy's personality quirks. If a person doesn't care enough to get to know these beautiful babies over the course of several weeks, why would she care about finding the right puppy for you?

The breeder should ask lots of questions about your lifestyle, experience with dogs, and reasons for wanting a Parson or Jack Russell Terrier. She might even decline to sell you a puppy because she thinks a Parson or Jack Russell is a poor choice for you or your current situation. You might disagree, and you might be right. On the other hand, if several people who are involved with terriers tell you the same thing, maybe you should reconsider your choice of breeds. Be glad that there are breeders who want their puppies and their buyers to live happily together.

Puppy Contracts and Guarantees

Many responsible breeders use puppy sales contracts to spell out the terms of the sale, including certain requirements incumbent on the buyer, and to protect themselves, the buyers, and the puppies. Sales contracts vary from one breeder to the next, so read the contract carefully and be sure you understand the terms. Consider having a disinterested, experienced breeder or exhibitor, or a solicitor, look at the contract before you sign.

A responsible breeder will allow you to see the mother of the puppy you are considering.

Your puppy should be guaranteed to be healthy when you take him home except for any condition noted in the contract. Most breeders cover the first 48 to 72 hours, during which time you should have your own vet examine the pup. Some breeders also offer "guarantees" against inherited diseases. Few breeders offer financial compensation, but many offer a "replacement." But dogs aren't interchangeable like refrigerators, so be sure you understand and are comfortable with the terms. Will you have to return the first puppy? Is there a time limit? Will the second puppy be closely related to the first? If you don't like the terms, or if the terms are unclear and the breeder won't clarify them *in writing,* look for another breeder.

It's important to understand that a puppy

guarantee *does not* mean that your puppy will never develop a problem. No one can guarantee that. On the other hand, it does mean that the breeder is confident about her breeding choices and will compensate you in some way if your puppy develops a problem. Your best bet is to buy from a breeder who screens her dogs for health problems and strives to breed healthy puppies, but you should also realise that with living things there's always some risk.

Pick of the Litter

Everybody and his brother has an opinion on the best way to choose *your* puppy. Your brother-in-law says you should let the puppy choose you. That might work, or you might end up with a dominant pup who's hard for you to handle. Someone else swears by puppy temperament and aptitude tests. Such tests are kind of fun, but they haven't been proven to predict adult behaviour accurately. Your best tool for selecting a puppy is a good breeder who watches and interacts extensively with her puppies for weeks and who listens to what you want and don't want in a dog. She can choose or help you choose the right pup based on much more information than you can get in one or two short visits.
If the final decision is up to you, watch the puppies play by themselves, with their dam and littermates, and with people. For most people, the pushiest puppy and the shyest puppy are not the best choices. A puppy who shows no interest in people may be more independent than you want. A prospective pet should be confident but not a bully, and he should be alert and interested in what's going on. Single encounters can fool you, though; if the puppies have played all afternoon, the one you think is calm and quiet may actually be a little fireball who just happens to be tired. That's why it's important to trust your breeder.

TESTING

American behaviourist Wendy Volhard has devised a temperament test that is designed for puppies around eight weeks of age. It is applicable to all breeds. It is a good idea to familiarise yourself with the tests so that you can try them out on your chosen puppy when you go to view a litter.

No matter the source of your dog, make sure that he is healthy.

Social Attraction

Place puppy in test area. From a few feet away, the tester coaxes the puppy to him/her by clapping hands gently and kneeling down. Tester must coax the puppy in a direction away from the point where he entered the testing area. The puppy is tested on the degree of social attraction, confidence or dependence.

Following

Stand up and walk away from the puppy in a normal manner. Make sure the puppy sees you walk away. The puppy is tested on the degree of following attraction. Not following indicates independence.

Restraint

Crouch down and gently roll the puppy on his back and hold him with one hand for a full 30 seconds. The puppy is tested on the degree of dominant or submissive tendency. How he accepts stress when socially/physically dominated.

Social Dominance

Let the puppy stand up and gently stroke him from the head to the back, while you crouch beside him. Continue stroking until a recognisable behaviour is established. The puppy is tested on the degree of acceptance of social dominance. Puppy may try to dominate by jumping and nipping, or is independent and walks away.

Elevation Dominance

Bend over, cradle the puppy under his belly, fingers interlaced, palms up, and elevate him just off the ground. Hold him there for 30 seconds. The puppy is tested on the degree of acceptance dominance while in position of no control.

Interpreting the Scores

Each test is scored individually, and a puppy may be assessed in points from 1 to 6. The scores are then evaluated as a whole.

- Mostly 1s: A dominant, aggressive puppy who resists human leadership.
- Mostly 2s: A dominant, self-assured puppy who accepts human leadership.
- Mostly 3s: An outgoing, friendly puppy who adjusts well.
- Mostly 4s: An easily controlled, adaptable puppy who looks to his master.
- Mostly 5s: An extremely submissive puppy who lacks confidence.
- Mostly 6s: An independent puppy who is uninterested in people.

For most owners, a good companion dog will score in the 3 to 4 range in this test. Puppies scoring a combination of 1s and 2s require experienced handlers.

ADOPTION OPTIONS

Older puppies and adult Jack and Parson Russells are always available to new homes. Let's see where they are.

Purebred Rescue Programmes

Rescue is the process of taking in and fostering homeless animals and then placing them in new homes when they're ready. Almost all rescuers are unpaid volunteers who donate time, knowledge, dog-handling skills, and living quarters as a labour of love.

Terriers find themselves in rescue for all sorts of reasons. Some

Most rescue dogs have no real problems, and they thrive when given the training, exercise, and care that they deserve.

have lost their owners to death, illness, or other misfortune. Some were unclaimed strays. Others have been removed from abusive situations. But the majority of terriers in rescue are there just for being what they are meant to be—smart, energetic, fearless, take-charge, working terriers who were in homes that couldn't manage their energy, intelligence, and other terrier traits. The typical rescued dog is an adolescent or young adult, although puppies or veterans are sometimes available. Most of the dogs have no real problems, and they thrive when given the training, exercise, and care they deserve.

Good rescue programmes will not place dogs with known histories of biting, aggression, or severe behavioural problems. They carefully evaluate each dog's temperament, behaviour, and training needs while he is fostered in a household environment.

Adopting a dog from a shelter can be rewarding, but proceed cautiously.

Groups vary, though, so be sure to ask about the procedures and policies of any group you contact. Volunteers usually begin basic training and encourage or require adopters to take their dogs to obedience classes. Rescued dogs are generally given physical examinations, and potential adopters are advised about possible health problems. Reputable rescuers always require that rescued dogs be neutered.

Adoption policies vary, but usually you'll have to fill out an application, provide references, and agree to a home visit. You'll sign an adoption contract agreeing to provide proper care and to return the dog to the organisation if you can't keep him. You'll pay an adoption fee or be asked for a donation. Please be generous—organised rescue programmes depend on private donations, and without such support they would cease to exist.

Don't forget to let your dog's rescuers know how he's doing from time to time. Knowing that a dog who passed through her hands is doing well and making someone happy is the rescue volunteer's best reward.

Questions to Ask When Considering Adoption

The following are some questions to ask if you're considering adopting an adult terrier.
- Why is he available for adoption?
- What can you tell me about this dog's history?
- Does he have any behavioural problems?
- Has he ever bitten or tried to bite anyone?
- Is he friendly with other dogs?
- How is he with cats (if you have a cat)?
- Is he housetrained?
- Has he had any training?
- Does he have any health problems that you know of?
- Has he had a physical examination and vaccinations?

Rescue Centres

Parson and Jack Russell terriers are in all-breed rescue centres for the same reasons they're in one-breed rescue programmes. The main difference is that in most centres, the dog will be one of many in a kennel situation, and no one will have the time or opportunity to observe the dog in a normal household situation. Adopting a dog from a rescue centre can certainly be rewarding, but proceed cautiously. If you're looking for a Parson or Jack Russell, but don't know the breed well, take someone with you who does. Most of the staff are dedicated animal lovers, but may not be able to identify breeds accurately. Mixed breeds can be great pets, but be sure that you know whether your dog is mostly or all Parson or Jack Russell.

When you find a dog who attracts you, ask about his known history, and how his temperament, training, and health status have been evaluated and by whom. If you are uneasy about the dog's behaviour, look for another dog. If you lack confidence in the rescue centre staff's ability to assess the dog and to give you knowledgeable advice, go to another rescue group.

The rescue centre should be clean. Dogs awaiting adoption may be thin and in need of a bath, but all should look fairly healthy. Some well-funded centres have all incoming animals examined by a vet, but many can't afford to offer more than basic evaluation and care. If you notice any signs of illness, like a runny nose or eyes, sores, lameness, and so on, be very cautious, no matter how sorry you feel for the dog. You don't want to bring home an infectious disease, especially if you already have a dog. If you want a specific

Reality Check

If you decide to adopt a dog from a rescue centre or other potentially stressful environment, take into account the effect the place might have had on the dog. He may be frightened or depressed.

Find out as much about the dog's past. While a stable home can bring out the best in him, you don't want to risk harming your family or anyone in your neighbourhood.

dog, but have concerns about his condition, take him to your vet for a thorough check and possible quarantine *before* you take him home. Many problems can be solved with proper food, exercise, and care, but it would be tragic if your good intentions harmed another dog in your home or neighbourhood.

The rescue centre makes it hard to see a dog at his best, because he may be lonely, depressed, or frightened. A little time in a quiet place and a few treats may help break the ice. The prospective adoptee should meet your whole family before you decide, but don't overwhelm a nervous dog with a rowdy crowd. Explain to your kids that the dog may be a little afraid—most kids are sympathetic, gentle, and quiet when they understand. Most terriers are outgoing and confident, so caution on the dog's part may not be an issue at all.

"Free to Good Home"

People sometimes have to find a new home for their dog. Sometimes they have good reasons, but be careful about dogs advertised in newspapers or on bulletin boards. An astonishing number of people have no qualms about "forgetting to mention" health or behavioural issues, including a history of biting. If lack of proper care or training is to blame, the dog may be fine in the right home. Some problems, though, are serious, so ask questions and pay close attention to the answers.

Ask specifically whether the dog has ever bitten, snapped, or threatened to bite a person, and whether he gets along with other animals. Listen carefully to the answer, and watch the person for signs that she might be stretching the truth a bit. Ask to see the dog's veterinary record. He should be up to date on vaccinations, worming and flea prevention, plus any other treatments that are needed, depending on where you live. If records are unavailable, call the vet who has seen the dog, explain that you are thinking of adopting, and ask if there's anything you need to know. If the dog has no history of health care, ask if you can have the dog examined by your own vet at your expense before you adopt him. Invite the owner to come, of course; she's unlikely to let you take the dog otherwise, especially if he's for sale rather than free. If there's no health-care record and you can't have the dog checked out, be alert and use your best judgment.

PUPPY PROOFING YOUR HOME AND GARDEN

Put potentially dangerous items out of reach of your inquisitive terrier.

Your new dog is coming home! Unfortunately, your home and garden can be dangerous as well as tempting for a puppy or even an older dog until he settles in. You need to get things ready.

Begin by putting attractive nuisances, breakables, and rip-up-ables out of reach to protect your new pup and your belongings. Dangling tablecloths or runners are tailor made for a terrier tug, and shoes, plants, and decorations will look like toys until your dog learns to leave them alone.

Gardens are full of toxins and other dangers, so keep your terrier out of gardens and compost. If you use chemicals on your lawn, follow directions for drying time before letting paws onto the grass. If you use a treatment, check with your vet about safety—don't rely on the people who sell or apply the chemicals for accurate information. Store poisons and antifreeze securely where your dog can't get to them, and clean any spills thoroughly. Dispose of containers for hazardous products where your dog can't get them.

Dogs sometimes swallow an amazing assortment of unlikely objects that can prove harmful or fatal, like pins, needles, wool, razor blades, cigarette butts, and nylon stockings. Chocolate, grapes and raisins, medicines, vitamins, and tobacco products can be lethal

as well. Teach your kids to put things away; they're usually more willing when the puppy's well-being is at stake (not to mention the well-being of any toys he may chew). Keep electrical and telephone wires out of reach, or run them through specially designed sheaths or PVC pipe to prevent chewing.

STOCKING UP FOR YOUR NEW TERRIER

You don't have to spend a fortune on puppy supplies, but some basic equipment and supplies will make your task of raising a puppy or settling in an adult dog a lot easier on both of you. Let's look at a basic shopping list.

Crate

Most experienced dog owners agree that the best tool for keeping your pup and your belongings safe, and the best tool for toilet training, safe travel, and confinement if the dog is injured or ill, is a crate (also called a carrier or cage). A crate will keep your dog (and your belongings) safe when you're not home, and it will keep him from doing things you don't want him to do. He will also be much safer travelling in a crate than he would be loose in a vehicle.

Dog crates come in wire, plastic, fabric and aluminum, on wheels, with handles, and in various colours and sizes. (Don't use a fabric crate until you're sure that your dog won't try to chew his way out.) A Russell needs a crate approximately 16 inches (40.6 cm) wide by 20 inches (50.8 cm) long. Be sure the door fits snugly and latches securely. You may want to provide bedding in the crate, but if your pup likes to tear things up, leave the bedding out until he outgrows his urge to rip.

Collar or Harness

Your dog needs at least one collar or harness. Many pet owners prefer to use a harness because the dog can't slip out of it, but for training you will need a collar. An adjustable, quick-release flat nylon collar is a good choice for a puppy. Nylon collars are inexpensive, come in a rainbow of colours, and are easy to readjust, which you will need to do frequently while your pup is growing.

Follow these practices to keep your dog safe while wearing a collar:

Dog Dens

Although you might not like to be confined to a small room, both wild and domestic canines often seek the security of small dens where nothing can sneak up on them. In fact, most dogs enjoy the den-like environment of their crates because it makes them feel safe.

- Don't leave dogs alone together wearing collars—one dog's collar can trap the other dog's jaw or leg, causing serious injuries to one or both.
- Adjust the collar so that you can insert two fingers between the collar and your dog's neck. Check the fit frequently and readjust or replace the collar when necessary.
- Don't use a slip (choke) collar on a puppy—you can severely damage his throat and spine.
- Never leave a slip collar on any dog when you're not actively training.

Lead

You also need at least one lead to control your dog every time he's outside your home or a securely fenced area. Don't underestimate how quickly your Russell can get away and be seriously hurt or killed. A 4- (1.2 m) to 6-foot (1.8 m) leather lead a quarter- (0.6 cm) to half-inch (1.3 cm) wide is strong and effective for control and training. Nylon leads are hard on hands and can burn or cut if a rambunctious dog winds them around your legs.

A crate is a great tool for toilet training, safe travel, and confinement.

Chain leads are ineffective for training and can injure you or your puppy.

Identification

Your dog should carry an identification tag with your phone number and your address on his collar. A permanent form of identification is a good idea, too, since collars and tags can be lost. Your veterinary surgeon can insert a microchip—a transmitter about the size of a grain of rice—under the skin over your dog's shoulders, or you can have your dog tattooed with an identifying number, normally on the belly or flanks. For more information, check with your vet.

Grooming Supplies

Your dog should carry his license tag at all times in case he becomes lost.

Although not a high-maintenance dog, your terrier will need some grooming supplies, including a brush, nail clippers and possibly a grinding tool or file, a mild shampoo formulated for dogs, and doggy tooth care products. You also may want a flea comb and a tick remover if those pests are a problem where you live.

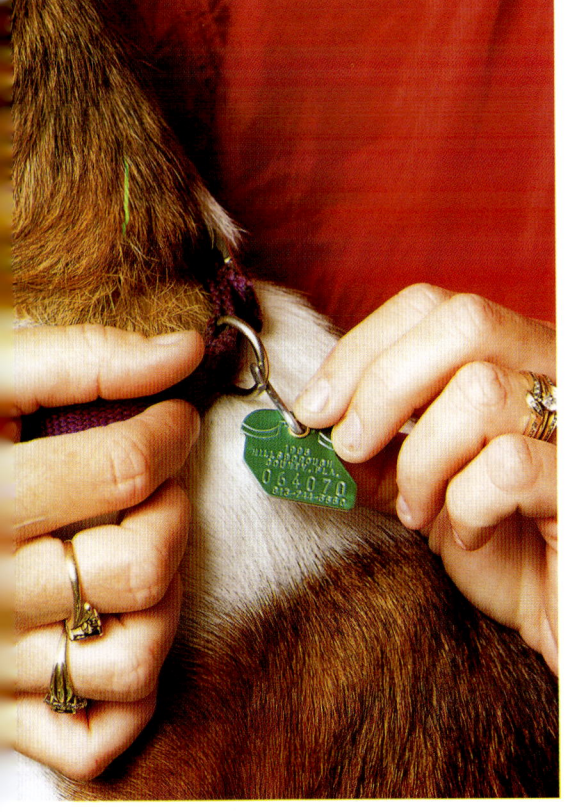

Toys and Chewies

You can have some fun choosing toys and chewies while you shop. Dogs have individual preferences, so if one toy goes unused, try another kind. Well-made chew toys, like Nylabone products, are safer and longer lasting than cheaper ones. Replace chew toys when they develop cracks or sharp points or edges or become too small to be safe. Terriers also like furry toys and squeaky toys, but dispose of damaged toys: Plastic eyes, synthetic stuffing, and squeakers can injure your dog if he swallows them.

Food

If you get your dog from a breeder or rescue group, they'll probably send some food home with you, but you'll need to buy more within a few days. Talk to your breeder, rescuer, or vet

about appropriate food for your dog. (See Chapter 4 for more information.) Treats in moderation are good for training, but too many treats can quickly make your dog fat, so give them sparingly, and keep an eye on your dog's weight. Many dogs also like carrots and small bits of fruits and other vegetables.

Food and Water Bowls

Your dog also will need bowls for food and water. Some dogs develop allergies to plastic bowls, and some ceramic bowls contain lead and other toxins that can leach into food and water. Stainless steel bowls are a good choice, because they are sturdy, easy to clean, and resistant to chewing.

YOUR TERRIER'S HOMECOMING

Most dogs settle into a new home quickly, but you can do a few things to make the process easier. Let's take a look.

Puppy's First Few Nights

If you're bringing home a puppy, he'll probably cry for attention and reassurance during his first few nights in your home. Remember that he's probably used to sleeping with his siblings, and now his whole world has changed. If you bring your puppy's crate into your bedroom at night, he'll feel more secure knowing you're nearby, and you'll be able to hear him and take him outside if he stirs.

Take your pup outside before bedtime. If he whines or barks in his crate, and you're sure he doesn't need to go, ignore him. At first he may complain for quite a while before he goes to sleep, but if he learns that complaining gets him nowhere, he'll quiet down. If you cave in and let him out, next time he'll be twice as loud for twice as long. If your puppy has been asleep and then cries, on the other hand, he probably needs to relieve himself. Carry him out, because he may not be able to hold it if he's walking. When he's finished, praise him and put him back to bed. You'll lose some sleep during the first week or two, but remember that your puppy is just a baby. How many babies do you know who don't keep their parents up for a few nights?

If your puppy can't sleep in your bedroom, expect him to cry the first few nights and to have a few accidents if you can't hear him asking to go out. Puppies' abilities to "hold it" between toilet

Shopping List

The following is a basic list of items you should considering purchasing for your new dog:
- Crate
- Dog bed or blanket
- Flat collar or harness
- Training collar if needed (ask your obedience instructor)
- Lead
- Toys and chewies
- High-quality food
- Food and water bowls
- Healthy treats
- Brush
- Nail clippers

Consider placing a ticking clock or a radio on low volume near your puppy's crate so that he doesn't feel completely alone.

breaks varies, but most puppies can go one hour for each month of age, plus one. So if your pup is four months old, he can probably go about five hours without urinating. Eight hours is about maximum for most adult dogs.

Living Nicely With Others

Dogs are not democratic. Left to their own devices, dogs in long-term groups or packs organise themselves into a dominance hierarchy. An alpha dog or bitch will be in charge, and every member of the group will occupy a specific rank, making him subordinate to pack members who rank higher and dominant over those who rank lower. Dominance is established mostly by force of personality and occasionally reinforced physically, not by age or sex or size. This hierarchical social system reduces conflict within the group because every dog knows his place.

Terriers, like many dogs, are territorial. Your dog will mark his territory—your home and garden—by urinating around the perimeter, and if you housetrain him properly, he'll mark only outdoors. Bitches (females) also mark territory, and some even lift their legs. Your dog also may defend his territory from intruders, which is why he barks at delivery people. If you already have a dog, he may see your new puppy or dog as an intruder and be less than welcoming, but you can reduce the friction with some planning. Generally, a male will accept a female and vice versa, and most dogs will accept a puppy more easily than an adult.

Introduce the dogs in neutral territory, where you don't usually take your dog, to reduce defensiveness. You need one person to handle each dog, and both dogs should be on lead for control. Let the dogs sniff each other while you talk to them in a quiet but happy voice. Watch their body language. If one dog lowers his front end in a bow and wags his tale, he's inviting the other to play. If one licks the other's mouth and chin, crouches, or rolls over on his back, he's displaying submission and acknowledging the other dog's higher rank—all good signs.

Less favourable body language includes hair standing on end, growling, bared teeth, staring, stiff-legged walking, or attempts by one dog to mount the other. If you see these signs of hostility, distract the dogs, move them apart, and have them sit or lie down to reinforce your position as alpha. Wait awhile, then try again. Keep encounters short and be alert. If the behaviour escalates, separate the dogs again. Some dogs don't like each other in the beginning but eventually become buddies, so don't give up too soon, but do be cautious. Dog fights can be violent, and injuries can occur if things get out of hand.

Be cautious for at least the first few weeks. When you can't supervise the dogs, separate or crate them. Many terrier owners say they never leave their dogs together when they aren't with them, because many terriers tend to be scrappy, and there's always the possibility of a fight, with consequent injuries.

If you're bringing home a puppy, don't leave him alone with an adult dog unless you're absolutely sure you can trust the adult. Even if you trust the older dog, give him time away from the puppy and private time with you. Puppies can be very annoying, and even a well-socialised adult can lose patience. Puppies younger than four months haven't mastered canine body language or manners and may not understand when older dogs tell them to back off.

If you have a cat, introduce a new adult terrier to her slowly and cautiously, and don't let the dog chase the cat. Don't force your cat to interact with the dog—let her initiate and control all encounters. If you have a puppy, teach him from the beginning that he may not chase or attack the cat. Give your cat dog-free areas where she can

Purchase only high-quality, well-made chew toys for your terrier.

sleep, eat, play, and use the litter tray without canine "assistance," and be sure she always has an escape route. Be aware, too, that some Russells simply can't resist the instinctive urge to chase and sometimes kill prey, which for some dogs includes cats.

ON THE ROAD WITH YOUR TERRIER

There will probably be many times when you want to take your terrier with you when you go out, which will most likely be just fine with your pet. If you keep a few precautions in mind, your terrier can safely accompany you on many trips, whether short or long in duration.

Don't leave your puppy alone with an adult dog unless you're absolutely certain you can trust the adult.

Travelling by Car

There's something very appealing about the sight of wind-blown ears and a lolling canine tongue appearing in a car window, but letting your dog travel loose in a vehicle is risky. Air-borne debris hitting eyes and ears at the speed of a moving vehicle can cause permanent damage. A leap from a window or the back of a truck can kill or injure your dog on impact or get him run over by another vehicle. An unrestrained dog can be thrown around if you hit the brakes, or he might go through a window in an accident.

Too much freedom isn't always a good thing for a travelling dog, but fortunately, a crate can keep your pup safe and secure when travelling. If you're in an accident, the crate will protect him from injuries and keep him secure in the aftermath.

More than one dog has survived a car accident and then been killed or lost when released through an open door. If you're hurt and unable to care for your dog, it will be much easier for someone else to do so if he's crated.

Another option is a doggy seatbelt. If it fits properly and is fastened securely, a seatbelt will keep your dog from being thrown around in an accident, although it won't protect him as well as a crate. Small dogs, like small children, can be injured or killed by a deploying air bag, so don't strap your terrier into the front seat, no matter how much you enjoy stroking his furry little head.

Anyone who has ever waited in a parked car on a warm day knows how quickly it can become uncomfortable, even with the windows slightly opened. For your dog, who cannot sweat and therefore has more difficulty cooling his body, it's even worse. In fact, the temperature in a parked car can become lethal for your dog in just a few minutes. If your dog won't be able to get out of the car with you on a hot day, leave him safe at home.

Your dog will be safer travelling in a crate than loose in the car.

Travelling by Air

In the UK, air travel was a rarity, but with the PETS Passport Scheme, it is bcoming an increasingly popular option. Your terrier can travel as cargo, or depending on the individual airline's regulations, in the cabin with you if he's in an airline-approved carrier that will fit under a seat.

A health certificate issued by a vet within ten days prior to the flight is required for all dogs travelling by commercial airline. Check well in advance with the carrier you plan to use for booking requirements, prices, restrictions, and so on.

Choose a pet sitter or boarding kennel that will give your dogs individual attention when you have to be away and they can't come with you.

If Your Dog Can't Come

Sometimes our dogs just can't come with us or are better off at home. Luckily, some good options are available for the stay-behind canine.

Boarding Kennels

If you choose carefully, a good boarding kennel is a safe alternative to taking your dog with you. Ask for recommendations, and tour the kennels ahead of time. Your dog should have a kennel run to himself unless you have asked to have two or more dogs housed together. The kennels and exercise areas should be clean, and fresh water always should be available. The entire kennel area should be fenced, so that if your dog slips out of his run, he'll still be confined. Plans should be in place to handle emergencies and to prevent theft or vandalism, and someone should be on-site at all times. Some kennels charge for extra services, such as extra play times or baths before departure, so be sure you understand what the basic service includes and how much the extras will cost.

Good Travelling Manners

All of us who love to travel with our dogs suffer the consequences of irresponsible behaviour by some people who have made our best friends unwelcome in some places. Most offensive are those who ignore lead requirements and let their dogs annoy other people and pets, and those who don't clean up after their dogs. It's hard to believe, but not everyone enjoys having a strange dog run up to visit, and no one likes close encounters with faeces. Picking up dog poop isn't the most pleasant thing we do for our dogs, but it's not difficult. A quick grab with a plastic bag or glove, a toss in the rubbish, and you're set. Please don't leave it for someone else.

If you stay in a hotel or other public lodging, please be courteous about your use of your room. Don't leave your dog alone to bark or cause problems, and bring a sheet to spread over beds or chairs where your dog may lie, so that you don't leave little white terrier hairs behind. Many dogs like to have their crates in hotel rooms—it's a little bit of home away from home.

Pet Sitters

Pet sitters are available to care for your dog at home. Some sitters come in a certain number of times each day, while others will stay in your home. Invite the prospective sitter to visit ahead of time to be sure she's comfortable with your pets and that you and your pets are comfortable with her. Ask how often she'll visit and what she's willing to do (like feed your dog, give medications, take him for walks, play, cuddle, groom, etc.). Ask about her experience with dogs (and other pets if you have any) and as a pet sitter. Ask whether she's affiliated with one of the national pet sitters' organisations and whether she has insurance. Has she had any special training, such as canine first aid? Does she have pre-planned procedures in case of emergency? Does she have a reliable vehicle? Can you check in with her while you're away? Get references and check them. Then, ask yourself if you'll be able to enjoy your trip without undue worry if this person cares for your dog, and follow your instincts.

Taking the time to choose your very own Parson or Jack Russell carefully and planning ahead for his arrival in your home will pay off in many ways. You'll be more confident that you've chosen the right breed and individual dog, and you'll be more comfortable about fitting your new dog into your home and lifestyle. Planning and shopping ahead of time will allow you to spend more time with your pup when you bring him home. Finally, knowing how to help your pup adjust to his new home and how to keep him safe and comfy whether you're home or not will help you rest easier. Now, have fun getting to know each other!

C h a p t e r

4

FEEDING

Your Parson or Jack Russell Terrier

Browse the shelves of any pet shop or supermarket, and you'll find commercial foods for dogs from every walk of life. Do a little research, and you'll find hundreds of books, websites, and Internet discussion lists that discuss raw and homemade diets. And you can be sure that no matter what you give your dog to eat, someone will be happy to tell you what's wrong with what you're feeding him.

With all of these types of diets and varying opinions, how can you ensure that your terrier's diet is healthy? You don't need a degree in nutrition, but you do need to choose intelligently and be aware that your dog really is, in part at least, what he eats. Learn the fundamentals of canine nutrition and how to evaluate your terrier's condition as it relates to his diet. Be aware, too, that if your dog develops a problem—lack of energy, dry skin and coat, itchiness, or chronic diarrhoea, for instance—it may be food related.

WHAT IS FOOD?

Like fine art, many of us can't define food, but we know it when we see it. It's useful, though, to understand what food is and how high-quality foods differ from "junk." Protein, fats, carbohydrates, vitamins, minerals, and water are the building blocks of food. The value of a food to specific animal depends on that animal's nutritional needs and on how well its digestive system processes that type of food.

Proteins

Proteins, found in meat products and plants, are composed of amino acids. To maintain good health, your dog needs to consume at least ten of the amino acids on a regular basis. Meat, fish, poultry, milk, cheese, yogurt, fish meal, and eggs are the best sources of complete proteins that have all the amino acids your dog needs, whereas plants provide incomplete proteins that lack some of the amino acids that dogs (and many other animals) require for optimum health. But that doesn't mean your dog should eat an all-meat diet; he needs vitamins and carbohydrates that meats lack, and a diet of only meat will cause your dog serious problems.

Fats

Meats, milk, butter, and vegetable oils also provide essential fats, which insulate your dog against cold temperatures, help cushion his internal organs, provide energy, and help carry vitamins and other nutrients through the bloodstream to his organs. Fat also makes food more palatable.

Although fats are necessary in your dog's diet, they shouldn't be excessive. Many low-priced dog foods are high in fat because it's cheaper than protein, and these foods may appear to provide proper nutrition for a while because fat provides energy. However, a long-term diet high in fat but lacking in proteins, vitamins, and minerals will eventually lead to symptoms of chronic malnutrition, so inexpensive foods are no bargain for your dog.

Carbohydrates

Carbohydrates, which are found chiefly in plants, provide energy. Corn, soya beans, wheat, and rice are common sources of carbohydrates in commercial dog foods. Because some dogs are allergic to one or more of these common grains, foods are also available that offer alternative sources of carbohydrates, such as potatoes.

Vitamins

High-quality dog foods provide vitamins in the proper amounts, and fruits and the livers of most animals are also rich source of vitamins, which are chemical compounds that support good health in several ways. Heat, light, moisture, and rancidity destroy vitamins, so food should be stored properly and used before its expiry date.

Protein, fats, carbohydrates, vitamins, minerals, and water are the building blocks of food.

Vitamins are essential for good nutrition, but be cautious about supplementing your dog's diet, especially if you're feeding him a good-quality dog food. Too much of a good thing is possible, and some vitamins are toxic in large amounts. Don't give your dog vitamin supplements unless your vet advises you to do so.

Minerals

Minerals build strong bones, strengthen cell tissue, and help your dog's organs function properly. Again, though, too high a mineral intake can damage your dog's health. A dog on a high-quality diet is extremely unlikely to suffer a mineral deficiency, and oversupplementation is a much more common cause of health problems in many dogs than is malnutrition. Never give your dog supplements containing calcium or other minerals, especially while he's growing, unless your vet advises you to do so. You could cause serious permanent damage to your pup's growing bones and tissues.

Water

We don't think of water as food, but adequate clean water is critical for life and good health. Your adult terrier's body is about 60 percent water, and puppies have even more water in their tissues. Like other animals, your dog takes in water directly by drinking, but he also uses metabolic water, or water released from food as it is digested. You may want to restrict late-night water consumption while housetraining your puppy, but otherwise your dog should have free access to clean water at all times.

Adequate clean water is critical to your terrier's good health

FOOD, TREATS, AND SUPPLEMENTS

Dogs are carnivores, and in the wild, their diets would consist mostly of prey animals. Take a look at your terrier's teeth, and you'll see that they are designed for that purpose. His long canine teeth ("fangs") are designed to slash and grasp his prey, and his molars are serrated and sharp and meet like the blades of a pair of scissors. They are designed for the purpose of shearing meat rather than for chewing vegetable matter. Although your dog and his wild cousins eat and enjoy fruits and vegetables, their digestive systems are designed primarily to handle meat proteins and cannot break down the cellulose walls of vegetable matter, so raw vegetables and fruits contribute very little food value to the canine diet. (Raw vegetables are terrific filler, though, for a dog on a diet.)

Wild carnivores eat not only the meat of their prey but also the partially digested vegetable matter in the stomachs of herbivores whose digestive systems are designed to handle grass, leaves, and other vegetation. Partial digestion makes the nutrients in the vegetables available to the carnivorous hunter, and for your homebound terrier, cooking does the same thing. Your dog may be a hunter at heart, but he still depends on you—or a manufacturer of high-quality dog food—to provide him with cooked vegetables so that he can utilise the nutrients they offer. Cooking, however, destroys some vitamins in food. Good commercial dog foods have vitamins added after the heat process is completed, and if you feed a homemade or raw diet, you'll probably need to include a vitamin supplement in your dog's daily rations. (Ask your vet for his recommendation.)

Now, let's take a closer look at the dietary options available for feeding your terrier.

Commercial Dog Foods

Walk down the pet food aisle of any pet shop or supermarket, and you'll find tinned foods, dry foods, semi-moist foods, foods for puppies and senior dogs, active dogs, couch potato dogs, fat dogs, healthy dogs, and dogs with dental problems. The protein sources in various foods may be beef, chicken, turkey, lamb, duck, venison, fish, or a combination of these things.

Prices of commercial dog foods vary widely, and while the most expensive isn't necessarily the best option for your dog, choosing a dog food by price alone could very well cost you more in the long run, both financially and emotionally. Low-quality ingredients, along with chemical preservatives and dyes used in some cheap foods, have been linked to serious health and behavioural problems, including cancers, allergies, and hyperactivity Besides, quality foods may cost more per pound than poorer ones, but your dog probably eats less, making the cost per meal about the same.

What makes a better quality dog food better? The ingredients, for one thing. Many of the better foods use meats and other foods suitable for human consumption, whereas lower priced foods do not. Better foods contain less filler, so they are nutritionally more dense and therefore more digestible—no small advantage if you have pooper-scooper duty or if you've lived with a gassy dog! Dogs who eat good diets also tend to have healthier skin, glossier coats, cleaner, healthier teeth and gums, and better overall health.

Dry Food

Dry, complete dog food comes in a wide variety of brands, qualities, and ingredients, and it is more convenient than other kinds of food. It requires no refrigeration, so it is relatively easy to store. Your dog's teeth and gums will stay cleaner on a diet of dry food because the food won't stick easily to his teeth, and it's more likely to scrape away tartar during chewing. If your dog is elderly or has trouble chewing, you can soften dry food with water, but that reduces the dental advantages of dry food. Your dog's stools will be firmer if he eats dry food; this is particularly true with high-quality dry dog foods, which are more digestible and contain less filler. Dry food is generally less expensive than semi-moist and tinned foods of equivalent quality.

Semi-Moist Food

Dogs with specific health problems may benefit from special formula foods.

Semi-moist dog foods are basically a soft version of a dry, complete diet. Semi-moist foods usually cost more than dry food, and they tend to stick to the teeth, potentially leading to gum disease. They often contain dyes and chemical preservatives that have been tied to health and behavioural problems in dogs. Frankly, your dog doesn't care what colour his food is as long as it tastes good, so why feed him food dyes? There really isn't much to recommend semi-moist foods.

Wet Food

Wet, or tinned, foods are relatively expensive, partly because you pay for the tin and the cost of shipping the water, which makes the food heavy. Quality tinned foods are good for dogs with certain dental or medical conditions, and they may be useful for enticing a dog whose appetite is poor due to old age or illness. However, for most dogs, a diet of tinned food only will probably contribute to tartar buildup, bad breath, flatulence, and soft, strong-smelling stools. Tinned food must be refrigerated once opened because it spoils quickly, and its strong fragrance tends to attract insects, so dishes must be washed soon after each meal.

Special Diets for Special Dogs

Dog food manufacturers offer a range of "special diets." Some are available through conventional commercial outlets, while others are sold only through veterinary clinics. Perhaps best known are the foods for puppies, senior dogs, overweight dogs, and very active dogs. These are usually simply variations on the "adult" or "maintenance" version of the same food, with often very slight differences in nutritional content, particularly protein and fat levels and sometimes vitamin and mineral content. Some formulas for seniors include supplements that are supposed to help fend off arthritis, and reducing formulas have fewer calories than their standard counterparts.

Are these "special" foods better than a high-quality adult dog food? That's debatable. Many vets and breeders prefer to feed adult food to puppies either from the day they begin eating solid food or from four to six months on, because too rich a food promotes growth that is too fast and can cause long-term health problems. As for senior formulas, there's no evidence that they are better than maintenance foods for the ageing dog, and supplements can be better controlled by adding them separately if needed. Reducing foods may have some value for getting weight off an obese dog quickly, but cutting back on the amount of regular adult food the dog gets will also do the trick. "Active" formula dog foods usually contain higher levels of protein and fat, and they can easily lead to

Dry 'complete' dog food will help keep your terrier's teeth and gums healthy.

Cooked Bones

Cooked bones splinter easily and can perforate your dog's intestines, causing serious injury and in many cases a painful death. Don't give your dog cooked bones, and be sure to keep rubbish safely out of reach.

obesity in dogs who don't really need the extra calories. A busy terrier may fool you into thinking he needs more food, but very few dogs are really active enough to need more nutrition than that offered by proper amounts of a good adult or maintenance food.

For a dog with specific health problems, special formula foods are worth the extra cost (and sometimes the trouble of finding them). If your dog develops an allergy to one or more ingredients commonly used in dog foods—beef, poultry, corn, soya, wheat, and preservatives in particular—then a food that uses an alternative meat source (duck, venison, and fish are common) and replaces the usual grains with oatmeal, potatoes, or other vegetable sources may be just what he needs.

Other special diets, available only through vets, are designed to support good health in dogs suffering from specific health problems, such as kidney disease. Special foods also are available that are supposed to help reduce tartar and keep your dog's teeth and gums cleaner and healthier, but before you spend the money, ask your vet about their value in maintaining your terrier's dental health.

Home-Cooked Diets

Many people feel that commercial diets contain questionable or inferior ingredients. If you're among that group, you may want to try feeding your dog a homemade diet. This should not, of course, be a haphazard fare of leftovers and table scraps, but a carefully planned diet made of healthy ingredients. Knowing what your dog is eating is one of the main attractions of the homemade diet, since you can use high-quality meat, poultry, and fish, as well as eggs and fresh-cooked vegetables and possibly grains.

A carefully designed homemade diet can provide excellent nutrition for your dog, but homemade diets have some drawbacks, too. You need to be sure that the food you make for your dog includes everything he needs to maintain good health. Your terrier doesn't need a complete balance of nutrients every day, but over the course of several days he needs to consume a proper balance of protein, carbohydrates, fats, essential fatty acids (found in fat/oils), minerals, and vitamins. This is especially critical for a growing puppy—poor nutrition during puppyhood can cause permanent damage that will affect your dog throughout his life. If you want to make your terrier's food, then learn as much as you can about

canine nutrition from reliable sources. A lot of opinions about homemade diets circulate among dog fanciers, especially on the Internet, and not all of them are based on research and facts.

A high-quality diet will make for a healthier dog.

One major disadvantage of a homemade diet is that you need a fair amount of time for planning, shopping, and preparation, and you need adequate storage space for ingredients. But if you like to cook and have the time to plan, shop, and prepare the food, and room to store the ingredients, then you may prefer to feed a homemade diet.

Raw Diets

Raw diets, sometimes known as Bio Active Raw Food or Biologically Appropriate Raw Food (BARF) diets, have become popular over the past two decades. Dr. Ian Billinghurst, an Australian vet and main advocate of the BARF diet, writes in his book *Give Your Dog a Bone* that dogs should eat a diet consisting of 60 percent raw meaty bones and 40 percent "a wide variety of human food scraps," mostly raw vegetables and fruits.

The bulk of the typical BARF diet is comprised of raw chicken and turkey bones, with periodic additions of organ meat (liver, kidney, heart, brain, tongue, and tripe) and eggs. Green leafy vegetables are included in the diet and are usually run though a food processor or juicer. Other additives often include vegetable oil, brewers yeast, kelp, apple cider vinegar, fresh and dried fruits, and raw honey. Some people give their dogs small portions of grain products, and some add dairy products, especially raw goat milk, cottage cheese, and plain yogurt.

BARF diets pose all the same time and storage problems mentioned earlier in regard to homemade diets. In addition, BARF-type diets pose a potentially more serious food-handling challenge. Raw meat, especially raw poultry, contains bacteria that cause food poisoning and can harbour parasite eggs and larva. If your terrier is generally healthy, his intestines will handle the bacteria without problems, although parasites can remain a threat. We humans, though, aren't so well protected. For your own safety and that of your family, it's critical that all counter spaces, cutting boards, knives, plates, and storage containers used for preparing raw foods be cleaned scrupulously after every use, and that you always wash your hands with soap and water after handling raw meat. Even better, wear disposable plastic gloves for the process, and wash well afterwards.

Treats

If you're like most dog owners, your terrier will get treats during training and at other times throughout the day. But be careful, because it's easy to add way too many calories to your dog's diet without realising what you're doing. The right kinds of treats are great in moderation and good for the souls of dogs and owners alike, but "treat abuse" will turn your dog into a Parson or Jack Russell Tubby.

The quality of your treats is very important. It is possible to give your dog a healthy treat that he also finds yummy, but choose treats as you would a dog food. Look for small or breakable treats—you should give morsels, not mouthfuls. If you plan to use the treats for training, you want something your dog can gobble quickly so that you can get back to the training, not wait around while he chews. Check the ingredients in treats, and avoid those that contain food dyes, and if possible, chemical preservatives. If your dog is allergic to a food item, such as corn, be sure there's none in his treats.

Be creative with your choice of treats. I've trained dogs with tiny bits of raw carrots and green beans, morsels of string cheese, and itsy bits of roast chicken and deli roast beef. Plain air-popped popcorn is fine for most dogs in moderation, although some are allergic to corn. A portion of your pup's daily dry food ration can also be used for treats; getting it one bit at a time seems to make standard fare much yummier.

Although a morsel once in a while won't do him any harm, avoid giving your dog most human treats. He may love crisps and crackers and such, but they're really not good for him. The grains and high fat content can cause allergic reactions, weight gain, and intestinal upsets, including flatulence and diarrhoea. Many dogs have a serious sweet tooth, but sugar is bad for canine teeth, and chocolate is toxic for dogs. Some fruits are fine in small amounts—little bits of apple, orange, banana, or berries, for instance—but raisins and grapes are toxic to dogs.

I know you love your dog, and he's so manipulative with those big brown eyes and the oh-so-grateful canine reaction to a handout, but even a few calories a day over his daily allotment can mean substantial weight gain for a dog the size of a Parson or Jack Russell Terrier. People tend to forget the treats they hand out, and they can't imagine how their dogs get fat on "just this much food." But treats do add calories, and if excessive, can throw off the nutritional balance of your dog's diet. There are many more healthy ways to show your dog you love him than by overdoing the treats.

Instead of using treats to distract your dog, try providing a variety of toys to exercise his body and mind.

Nutritional Supplements

In our "take a pill" society, a vast assortment of doggy pills and supplements are widely available and largely unregulated. You can find dietary supplements that are supposed to calm your dog down, perk him up, make him shed less, give him a prettier coat, stop his itching, drive away fleas, make him grow, make him thin—you name it! Some supplements probably do help some dogs, but the claims made for many of them are at best unfounded and at worst potentially hazardous to your dog's health, not to mention your wallet.

If your dog eats a balanced, healthy diet, it's doubtful that he

To prevent obesity in your terrier, monitor his food intake and make sure he gets plenty of exercise.

will need supplements, and some supplements can harm him. Excess calcium, for instance, can contribute to kidney stones and other problems in adult dogs, and in puppies, it can cause serious problems with bone growth that will affect the dog throughout his life. Hypervitaminosis (too much vitamin intake) is not uncommon in dogs who are given dietary supplements, and some vitamins, especially A and D, are toxic in large amounts. In addition, many vitamins must be ingested in proper ratios to other nutrients to be effective. Your best bet is to avoid giving your puppy or dog nutritional supplements unless your vet advises you to do so.

HOW MUCH TO FEED

Obesity is as big a problem in dogs as it is in people, and the typical adult pet terrier is overweight. People often plead that they can't understand why their dogs are fat, but except in very rare cases of metabolic disease, the reason is simple—a fat dog is a dog who eats too much. In fairness to softhearted owners, most dogs will plead starvation most of the time and will eat whatever they can wheedle out of people. This opportunistic appetite makes sense for a wild canid; a predator never knows for sure when he'll eat his next meal, so he eats what he can when it's available. But for the modern pet, regular meals and food aplenty make the advantages of pigging out obsolete.

Commercial dog foods always list recommended portions on their packages, but these should be used as very loose guidelines only. The amounts are often considerably more than the average dog needs to maintain a healthy weight. Whatever your dog is eating, monitor his weight and condition throughout his life. It's easy to get into a pattern and continue to scoop up the same amount of food year after year, but your dog's nutritional needs will change over time. As a growing puppy, your dog will need more food than he'll need as an adult, and as he ages he may need more or less food, depending on his health and activity levels.

Your terrier's general health and physical appearance are the best indicators of whether his diet suits him. If he's neither skinny nor fat, is alert and active as appropriate for his age, and has a glossy coat and healthy skin, then his diet is probably fine. Improper weight, lethargy, poor skin and coat, disinterest in food, changes in eating habits, and unexplained weight changes can indicate health problems, so if you notice any of these signs in your dog, see your vet. If your dog is healthy but picks at his food or leaves some, cut back on the amount you're giving him. If he still won't eat, consider trying a different food—some dogs simply don't care for a particular food. If he gains or loses weight when he doesn't need to, adjust the amount of food you give him, and if his skin and coat aren't healthy but his general health checks out, consider changing his food. Don't forget to include treats when you calculate his daily consumption—those calories count, too!

How to Check for Excess Weight

To check your dog for excess weight, run your index finger and thumb along the ridge of his spine from his shoulders to his tail. You should be able to feel his ribs without pressing down. When you look down at your dog's back, you should see a "waist" or narrowing behind his ribs.

WHEN TO FEED

There's a widespread misperception that free-fed dogs—dogs who have free access to food at all times—don't get fat. Unfortunately, free feeding often does lead to obesity, especially in multidog households, where each dog may eat more, and more often, to beat his "competition" to the food. Scheduled feeding, in contrast, lets you control your dog's daily food intake, and therefore his weight, much more easily than free feeding does. Scheduled feeding also makes it easier to monitor your dog's well-being. Lack of appetite is often the first sign that your dog is ill, and if you free feed him, you may not notice right away that he's not eating.

Practical issues must be considered, too. Free feeding will make the housetraining process more difficult because scheduled meals make for more regular toileting, whereas a random eating schedule leads to unscheduled toilet breaks. Free feeding can also interfere with obedience training, especially if you use food treats to

Good nutrition provides the fuel your terrier needs to grow and develop properly as a puppy and adolescent.

motivate and reward your dog. If he can eat whenever he wants to, training treats won't be as interesting as they would be if food were harder to get. Free feeding is also impractical if you are travelling with your dog, and if you board him while you're away, he'll likely be fed on schedule, making that one more change he'll have to deal with. Finally, food that's left out may attract animals and insects to your dog's bowl, and it may become dirty or spoiled if it's out too long.

Water, on the other hand, should be readily available at all times. The only exceptions to free access to water are when you are housetraining a puppy (you might want to remove water a couple of hours before bedtime); before anaesthesia; and occasionally for other reasons as advised by your vet.

FEEDING YOUR TERRIER FOR LIFE

The best number of meals and times to feed them depend in part on your schedule and in part on your terrier's age. There's no single "correct" approach to feeding, but some general guidelines do apply to feeding dogs at different stages in their lives.

Feeding Your Puppy

A quick way to get an enthusiastic debate going among breeders, fanciers, veterinary surgeons, and nutritionists is to ask how to feed a puppy. Some breeders require that their puppies be fed a certain way—a particular dog food or a raw or homemade diet, for instance—for their contractual guarantees to be valid. If that doesn't apply to your pup, then consider the information in this book along with advice from your breeder and your vet and from other legitimate written sources so that you can make an informed decision.

One of the debates focuses on whether puppies should be fed "puppy food." Most commercial puppy foods contain extra protein and calcium to promote faster bone growth, but research shows that puppies don't need the extra nutrients. Puppy food probably won't hurt your pup, but he'll also probably do just as well on a high-quality adult or maintenance food. In any case, if you do feed puppy food, most vets and breeders recommend that you switch to adult formula when your puppy is about four months old. If you have opted to feed a raw or homemade diet, talk to your vet, or better yet, a veterinary nutritionist, about the diet. Lack of complete nutrition during the growth phase can affect your dog for his entire life, and excess amounts of some nutrients can also cause long-term damage—calcium supplements in particular are notorious for causing permanent damage to growing bones and joints. *Never* add calcium or other minerals to a growing puppy's diet unless advised to do so by your vet.

Breeders approach the weaning of puppies in different ways. Some "force wean" the pups sometime between four and six weeks of age, meaning that they remove the mother from the pups and feed them regular food, usually made into a "soup" initially. Other breeders allow a more natural weaning process to take place, with the puppies determining when they want to try mum's food, and letting mum decide when she's had enough of the sharp little teeth pulling on her teats. Whichever way your pup was weaned, by six to seven weeks of age, he was probably eating mostly or entirely "real" food three or four times a day and has learned to drink water to take the place of mum's milk.

When you pick up your puppy, your breeder should tell you what and when he's been eating, and she will probably send home a few days' supply of food as well. Ask your breeder's advice on

Loss of Weight or Appetite

If your dog's lack of interest in his food persists, or if he's losing weight, take him to the vet. Loss of appetite or unexplained weight loss can indicate serious illness.

Scheduled feeding allows you to control your dog's daily food intake.

feeding your growing terrier. In general, puppies from 7 to 16 weeks of age need three meals a day. Their nutritional needs are high because they are growing quickly, but their stomachs are too small to hold all the food they need in just one or two feedings. If possible, space meals evenly during your waking hours, with the last one several hours before bedtime to allow time for pre-bedtime toileting. If evenly spaced meals aren't practical for your situation, you may need to adjust the meal schedule. In any case, your pup needs a morning meal, a noon or afternoon meal, and an evening meal. From 16 weeks onwards, your pup needs two meals a day. Monitor your puppy's growth and weight gain carefully, and adjust his food intake as necessary to maintain growth without letting him get fat.

Regularly scheduled meals will help establish a routine and will make housetraining go much more easily. The specific times aren't important, so fit mealtimes into your schedule. However, allow at least half an hour after the meal, and take your pup out to relieve himself before you crate or confine him. When your pup is older and reliably housetrained, his feeding schedule doesn't need to be quite so rigid.

Feeding Your Adolescent

During his first few months, your puppy will eat about twice as much food as he'll need as an adult, but as he approaches full growth, he'll need less food, and he'll be able to eat just one or two meals a day. During adolescence, he should show good bone and muscle development and be well covered with flesh, neither skinny nor fat. He should also be active and alert, and his coat should have a healthy shine. Keep a close eye on his condition and adjust his food as needed.

Adolescence is a time of changes for dogs, as it is for people, and as we'll see later in this chapter, food can be an excellent tool for guiding your dog through this challenging period with training.

Feeding Your Adult

As your dog moves from adolescence into adulthood, his metabolism will change, and he may need fewer calories per day, even if he remains very active. Weigh your dog regularly, and remember that even half a pound (0.2 kg) is a significant weight change on a dog the size of a Parson or Jack Russell Terrier. You can respond more effectively to changes if you catch them quickly.

Some people feed their adult dogs once a day, some twice. Twenty-four hours is a long time to go without a meal, so I prefer and recommend morning and evening meals. However, many dogs adjust to once-a-day eating, so you'll need to decide what works best for you and your dog.

Food is a factor in many health and behavioural problems, and all too often, people spend lots of money on treatments that would be unnecessary with a simple change of diet. Food allergies, in particular, can easily go undiagnosed because they can develop over time. Your dog may do fine for several years on a food that contains corn, for instance, and then suddenly develop an allergic skin condition. If you suspect that food is causing your dog a problem, your vet may be able to guide you. Be aware, though, that many traditional vets are not trained in nutrition and don't necessarily think of food as a factor when health problems arise. Before resorting to steroids and other drugs, consider taking your dog to a holistic vet or a veterinary allergist, or do some research of your own on food allergies, and try switching your dog to a food that doesn't contain the suspected ingredient.

Obesity-Related Health Problems

Obesity contributes to serious health problems, including:
- Heart disease
- Diabetes
- Pancreatitis
- Arthritis
- Respiratory problems

How to Slow Down a Food Gulper

Does your dog eat like there's no tomorrow, gagging and choking in the process? Here are some ways to slow him down:

- Put his dry food in a toy designed to release a few pieces at a time as he bats it around. (There are several of these on the market.)
- Toss his dry food on the floor for him to pick up. You can combine this approach with training.
- Put a few clean 2- (5.1 cm) to 3-inch (7.6 cm) rocks in his bowl so that he has to pick the food from among them. (Be sure the rocks are too big for him to swallow.)

Feeding Your Veteran

Most dog food companies now offer "light" and "senior" foods for older dogs. Most of these foods contain less protein and fewer calories than adult or maintenance foods, and some also have supplements that are supposed to be good for older, arthritic dogs. This all sounds great, but no scientific evidence shows that geriatric foods offer older dogs any more benefits than a high-quality maintenance food. If your senior terrier is healthy and in good condition, there's no particular reason to change his food just because he's ageing. You might want to offer him certain supplements to support ageing joints and organs, but again, do so only with your vet's approval.

Have you ever noticed that food doesn't taste as good when your nose is stuffy, and you can't smell the aroma? The same thing may happen to your senior terrier if his senses of smell and taste are no longer as acute as they used to be. If he seems to lose interest in his food gradually, and is otherwise healthy, you may be able to make his food more appetising for him. Be sure your dog's food is room temperature or a bit warmer (but not hot), because it will be more fragrant when warm. If you feed dry food, a little warm water or unsalted stock added a few minutes before mealtime will bring out the fragrance and soften the food to make it easier to chew. Sometimes adding a little something special will make food more interesting, too. A spoonful of cottage cheese, plain yogurt, or high-quality tinned dog food mixed into your dog's dry food may be all it takes to get the oldie eating again.

If your dog suddenly stops eating, check his teeth, gums, tongue, and roof of mouth for injuries or foreign objects. If his teeth are discoloured or his gums look inflamed, schedule a professional tooth cleaning with your vet. Regular mouth care should be part of your terrier's grooming routine throughout his life, but it becomes especially important in old age.

Another potentially serious problem for many ageing dogs is dehydration. Try to keep track of how much he drinks each day, and if your terrier has trouble getting around or just doesn't feel well, try to make fresh water more easily available. If he spends a lot of time upstairs in the bedroom or in the basement family room, the stairs may be more trouble than a drink is worth, so think about placing an extra water bowl or two where he can get to them more easily. If your old friend has become really immobile, you might carry some water to him occasionally. Be sure to change the water in the bowl at least daily, and wash the bowl regularly to remove mineral deposits. Granted, dogs eat and drink all sorts of yucky stuff, but even so, don't ask your best friend to drink something you wouldn't drink. If you suspect that your older dog is not drinking properly for more than a day or so, talk to your vet.

Don't let your elderly terrier put on weight, which he may do if his food intake stays the same, but his activity and metabolism slow down. In addition to good nutrition and adequate water, be sure your dog gets some suitable exercise as he ages. Older dogs still enjoy daily walks and reasonable games like fetch the ball, and if your dog likes the water, swimming is good exercise for old joints. Just don't let him swim when the water or the weather is very cold. Whatever activities he continues to pursue, don't let your dog exhaust or injure himself, because he may not be willing to admit that he's no longer a youngster. It's up to you to protect him from himself! Fortunately, as long as your ageing dog is reasonably healthy, moderate activity will help maintain his muscle tone and proper weight, and help prevent depression.

PREVENTING OBESITY

Food makes most dogs happy, and making your dog happy makes you happy, so why not show him how much you love him by feeding him what he wants? Who cares if he's a bit pudgy as long as he's happy?

Unfortunately, obesity leads to serious problem in dogs, as it does in people. Being overweight will make daily doggy life more difficult. Your dog won't be able to run as fast or jump as high without hurting himself, he'll overheat more easily, and he'll tire out more quickly. He won't even be able to curl

Your dog will only get enough exercise if you spend time playing with or walking him.

up into a nice little doggy ball for a nap. Obesity can also contribute to serious health problems and shorten your dog's life.

Your dog is what he eats. Good nutrition provides the fuel your terrier needs to grow and develop properly as a puppy and adolescent. Good nutrition also helps keep him healthy and fit and promotes mental and emotional health from puppyhood through old age, helping him live and stay active longer.

Too many pet dogs are overweight, and most of their owners claim they don't know how their dogs got so fat. As we've seen, though, excess weight is nearly always caused by overeating. A number of factors determine your dog's individual nutritional requirements:

Your dog's weight is something you need to monitor over the course of his entire life.

- *Activity Level*—The more active your dog, the more food he needs.
- *Quality of Food*—The more nutritionally dense your dog's food, and the more easily he can digest it, the less he needs.
- *Age*—Your dog will need more food as a puppy than he'll need as an adult, and he'll need more while he's young and active than he will when he slows down later in life.
  - *Health Status*—Your dog may need more food, or specific foods, while he's recovering from an injury, surgery, or illness than he does at other times.
  - *Individual Variation*—Each dog's nutritional needs are his and his alone. Two terriers of the same age and lifestyle may need different amounts of food to stay at a healthy weight.

Hopefully, your dog will carry the proper amount of weight from puppyhood through old age, but sometimes an extra pound or two sneaks on before we notice. If your pup gets too much padding, you can do a number of things to help him take it off.

Measure Your Dog's Meals

Many people feed portions that are bigger than they think they are, so to prevent this from happening, measure your dog's meals using a standard measuring device. It's awfully easy to get into the habit of scooping "one serving" without realising that your scoop is closer to two servings. Also, keep track of your dog's daily intake of treats. If you're not sure how much you've been giving him, try measuring out treats

for the day and limit your dog to those. (Be sure other family members are following the programme, too.) You might even set aside part of your dog's regular daily portions to use as treats; the food is special when handed out one little bit at a time, and the "treats" won't add calories to his diet.

When your Russell becomes an adult, he will need fewer calories than he did as an adolescent.

Reduce Food Intake

If your dog has already put on some extra weight, simply reducing his food intake is another way to slim him down. If you're like a lot of dog owners, though, you may find it hard to resist your dog's pleas for more food. Luckily, some diet tricks will help your pudgy dog feel more satisfied and still take the weight off him. If you feed dry dog food, soak a quarter of the meal in water until it's soft, because the soaked pieces will expand and be more filling. At meal time, mix half his regular dry portion with the soaked food and serve; your dog will eat a fourth less food, but it will seem like more. You can also cut back on your dog's regular food and add low-calorie, high-fibre food to his diet. Some popular choices are unsalted green beans (fresh are fine), shredded or sliced carrot, lettuce or spinach, tinned pumpkin (plain, not pie filling), or air-popped unsalted popcorn. (Don't use popcorn if your dog is allergic to corn.) If your dog isn't used to getting vegetables, it may take him a few meals to develop a taste for them, but most dogs eventually do. If

Food, Glorious Food

Just like humans, dogs enjoy eating — both their regularly scheduled meals and all the extra treats that come their way. They soon figure out who will give them what they want, and they can turn into convincing beggars. To reinforce manners and keep begging at bay, turn giving food into training time. Ask your terrier to sit before putting his food bowl down. Going to his bed or crate while you eat and staying there quietly can earn him healthy leftovers. He won't mind "working" for food.

these approaches don't work, ask your vet about a weight-loss or lower-calorie food.

Have Your Dog Tested for Thyroid Function

You might also have your dog tested for proper thyroid function, but most obesity is due to nothing more than taking in more calories than the animal burns. Some people think that a high-energy dog will naturally stay slim, but that's often not true. The effort it takes to adjust your dog's diet to keep him at a proper weight is a small price to pay to help him live a longer, healthier, happier life.

FOOD AND THE SOCIAL ANIMAL

As we all know, food and meals are important aspects of social behaviour among our own species. The same is true for dogs. The most basic canine social principle related to food is that control of food is a sign of social dominance. You can use this simple fact to your advantage if you understand and use it properly.

Managing Your Dog With Food

One of the most common—and most serious—behaviour problems in dogs is what behaviourists call *resource guarding*, the animal's attempt to keep a resource to himself, often by threatening or using force.

Dogs regard food as an extremely valuable resource, and some dogs try to control food by guarding it, particularly from other animals and children. Guarding may begin with a growl, but if allowed to continue, the behaviour may escalate until someone is bitten. (For more on preventing and stopping resource guarding, see Chapter 6.)

You Gonna Eat All That?

Most dogs are natural-born beggars, and most people who like dogs are easy targets. What many people fail to understand, though, is that dogs also know that life isn't fair, and if raised and trained properly, they accept that they can't always have what they want. It's your job to teach your dog a couple of important life-shaping principles. First, you need to teach him that staring and begging won't get you to hand over your food. You can teach this by refusing to reward your dog for begging. If begging never works, he'll stop doing it. This is a case in which "never" really does mean never. If you occasionally reward your dog with just a taste, he'll be even more persistent next time. And terriers are nothing if not persistent! Whether you're snacking in front of the TV or eating dinner at the table, if you don't want a perpetual pest, teach your dog to lie down and mind his own business whenever you or anyone else is eating.

I'm not really that stingy with my own dogs, and you can sometimes share without turning your best buddy into a nuisance. Wait until you've finished eating, take your dog to another area, and have him do something—an obedience command or a trick— and reward him with the treat. In fact, this can be a good way to reinforce training, as we'll see in Chapter 6. Food is like currency for your terrier—he can learn to "work" for food, and become a better behaved, happier companion at the same time.

The old saying "You are what you eat" applies as much to your terrier as it does to you. Feeding a high-quality diet, whether commercial or homemade, keeping your dog at a healthy weight, and paying attention to the social uses of food will help your dog live a longer, healthier, happier life.

If your dog has put on extra weight, one way to slim him down is to reduce his food intake.

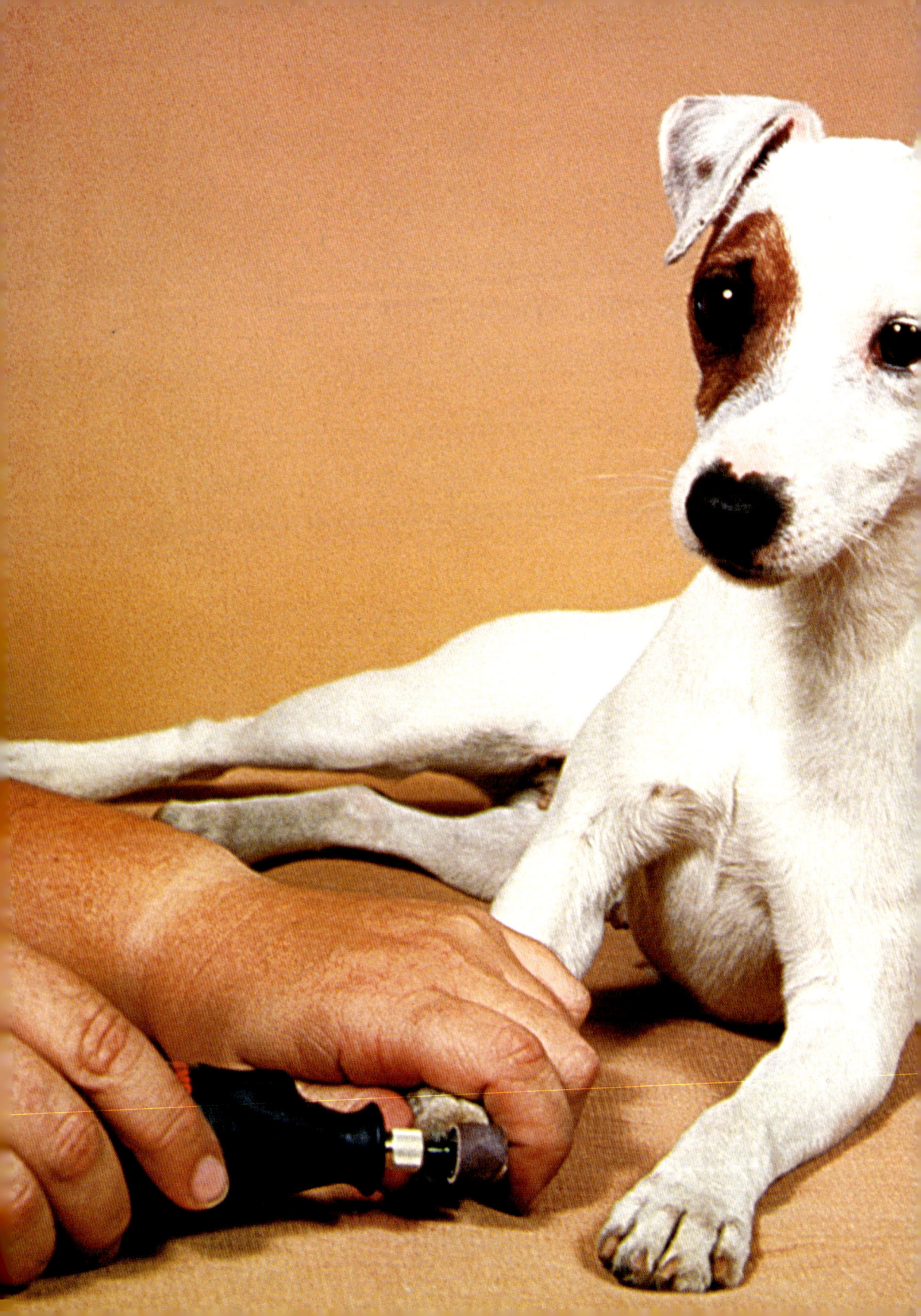

Chapter

5

GROOMING

Your Parson or Jack Russell Terrier

Although your terrier doesn't require hours of brushing or trimming like some dogs, grooming is still an important part of caring for your dog. Let's see why grooming is important and how you can make your terrier look his best.

WHY SHOULD YOU GROOM YOUR TERRIER?

If Parson and Jack Russell Terriers are essentially wash-and-wear dogs, why is grooming important? One good reason is that grooming sessions are special times for you and your dog. If you're gentle, and if you talk to your dog while you groom him, he'll learn to love the feel of your hands on his body, just as you love the feel of his fur against your skin. Your dog will also learn to trust your hands, which is important in training and vital in an emergency. If you teach your dog to accept and enjoy being groomed, the chances are both of you will find grooming sessions to be relaxing and gratifying.

Your terrier's health will benefit from regular grooming, too. He'll obviously be cleaner as a result, but at least as important, grooming sessions give you a chance to check him for cuts, bites, bumps, sore spots, and other early signs of health problems that you might not otherwise notice until they become serious.

Brushing removes lots of loose hair that would otherwise end up on your furniture, floors, carpets, and clothes, and trimming nails makes them less likely to scratch floors or snag carpets or upholstery, thereby helping to minimise the additional housework that's part of living with a dog—even a wash-and-wear little terrier.

COAT CARE

Your terrier's weatherproof coat is low maintenance, but to look and feel his best, your dog will still need some coat care. The details of how to do this will depend on whether your dog has a smooth or a broken coat.

Brushing

The smooth Russell has a dense outer coat of short, coarse hair that lies flat to the body. Ideally, the outer coat feels "hard," the texture helping it repel water and shed dirt more

Grooming Supplies

The following are some supplies that you will need to groom your Parson or Jack Russell Terrier:
- Slicker brush for cleaning the coat and removing loose hairs
- Nail clippers
- Optional nail grinder for grinding nails
- Mild shampoo formulated for dogs
- Doggy tooth care products

readily. The outer coat overlies a thick, plentiful undercoat, which protects the skin and keeps the dog warm and dry regardless of weather. The smooth-coated Russell sheds quite a lot—you can expect to find short, coarse hairs clinging to carpets, upholstery, and clothes. You can keep loose hair under control and keep your terrier's coat clean and shiny by brushing him regularly with a firm-bristle brush or a slicker brush, which has tiny metal teeth set into a flat backing.

The broken-coated or rough-coated terrier also has a double coat. His undercoat is like that of his smooth cousin. His outer coat consists of a smooth jacket that lies flat over his back and sides, and longer hair on his belly, legs, and face. This longer hair tends to be wavy or curly. If you show your broken- or rough-coated terrier in conformation, he'll have to be hand stripped, or plucked of loose hairs, every six to eight weeks. If he's not being shown, he can be clipped, which will soften his coat.

To remove loose hairs and dirt from your terrier's coat, brush him gently from front to back with short strokes of the slicker brush. Don't press too hard, because you can scrape his skin with the pins of the brush!

If you think your dog may have picked up some fleas, comb through his hair with a flea comb, paying special attention to the hair behind his ears and above his tail. The narrow spaces between the teeth of the comb will trap any fleas that are hitching a ride, and you can take action before the problem gets out of hand.

Bathing

You'll undoubtedly want to bathe your terrier occasionally—more frequently if he's active outdoors and gets himself grubby and smelly, as dogs like to do. However, doggy bath time doesn't have to be a test of wills and quick reflexes if you take the time to teach your dog that being bathed isn't such a terrible thing to endure.

Start training your dog for baths as soon as you bring him home, which will hopefully be before you need to bathe him. To teach him to accept the bath or sink, put him in it, give him a treat, praise him, and pet him gently. If he struggles to get out, hold him there gently but firmly, and talk to him quietly. When he stops struggling, take him out of the bath. Don't reward him or make a fuss about him after he's out; the idea is to teach him that he gets rewards for being in the bath, not for getting out. Repeat this process once or twice a day for a while, slowly increasing the time he has to stay in the bath. When he's comfortable in the dry bath, add a little lukewarm water so he gets his feet wet, and continue to reward him while he stands in the water. When he's comfortable with having his feet in the water, wet his body with lukewarm water from a sprayer or by pouring water onto him from an unbreakable container, again rewarding him for accepting it. This process takes some time and planning, but if you follow through, your dog will accept bath time without fear, and he may even enjoy being bathed.

Now it's time for a real bath. Gather everything you need before you start—you don't want to discover you need a towel from the linen closet when you have your sopping-wet dog in the bath. Here's what you need:

- Dog shampoo
- Cotton-wool balls
- Ophthalmic ointment
- Nonslip mat
- A hose or unbreakable container for rinsing
- One or two towels
- Hair catcher for the drain

Before you wet your terrier, brush your dog to remove loose hair. Place a cotton-wool ball into the opening of each ear to protect the ear canal against water. (Don't push it in too far.) Soap can cause soap burns, so apply an ophthalmic ointment (available from your vet, groomer, or pet supply store) to your dog's eyes to protect them, or be *very careful* not to get soap into his eyes. If you do, rinse his eyes thoroughly with clean water. When you have everything you need close at hand, put your dog into the bath or sink and reward him as you did in training.

Use lukewarm water to thoroughly wet your dog, then apply shampoo and work it in

A slicker brush will clean your terrier's coat, as well as remove loose hairs.

Flea Removal

If your dog has fleas, you don't need insecticidal shampoo to kill them. Using regular dog shampoo, wet and lather your dog thoroughly. Begin with a "collar" of lather high on his neck to keep any fleas leaving his body from hiding in his ears, and then lather the rest of his body. Leave the lather on for about 10 minutes to drown the fleas, and then rinse.

with your fingers, beginning at your dog's neck and working towards the tail. (Be sure to use a shampoo formulated for dogs, because shampoo for people will dry and damage your dog's skin and coat. Special shampoos are available for certain skin conditions, but unless your vet recommends one, all you need is a good-quality mild shampoo.) Don't forget his belly, up under his hind legs, and under his tail. You can save money and make lathering and rinsing easier if you dilute your dog's shampoo before you apply it. Mix one part shampoo with one or two parts water in a clean squirt bottle, shake well, and apply a small amount of the mixture to your dog. Don't lather your dog's face—use a washcloth for more control, and avoid his eyes.

Soap residue can irritate your dog's skin, so be sure you rinse him thoroughly. Go over his body with your hands after rinsing to be sure you got all the soap, and pay particular attention to his armpits, under his hind legs, and the groove along his belly between his ribs where soap loves to hide. When you're sure all the soap is out, gently squeeze the excess water from your dog's coat. Then, rub him vigorously with a towel, finishing up by smoothing his fur in the direction of growth.

Keep the end of the bath calm and controlled, because you don't want your dog to make a desperate bid for freedom and hurt himself in the process. Also, be sure to praise and reward your dog *before* you release him. The reward is for being good in the bath, not for escaping from it. You also may find that it's a good idea to put a collar and lead on before removing your dog from the bath; many wet dogs have "crazy dog attacks" in which they run and roll and

Causes of Bad Doggy Odour

Your dog shouldn't smell bad or have bad breath. Offensive doggy odours are usually caused by one or more of several causes:

- Oil, bacteria, or yeast on the skin
- Ear infections
- Impacted or infected anal glands
- Gum disease or tooth decay
- Intestinal or stomach gas
- A foreign substance on the coat and/or skin

If your dog smells bad, follow your nose to the source, work with your vet if necessary, and fix it. You'll be happier, and your dog will be healthier.

rub themselves on things (carpets, walls, furniture, bedspreads, etc.). You might want to confine your dog to a particular room or his crate until he's dry, and be sure to keep him warm and out of drafts. If he needs to go out, take him on lead, because wet dogs love to roll in the dirt! If you want to speed up the drying process, you can blow-dry your dog, but use a cool setting to avoid drying out his skin and coat.

If you plan to show your Parson or Jack Russell Terrier in conformation shows, ask his breeder to teach you to bathe him and care for his coat so that you don't damage its texture, which can hurt him in competition.

You will need to bathe your terrier more frequently if he is especially active outdoors.

HEALTHY FEET AND NAILS

Have you ever tried to walk with sore feet or ill-fitting shoes? Nails that are allowed to grow too long make your dog's feet feel the same way. Check your dog's feet frequently, especially between his toes and pads where burrs, stones, small sticks, and other debris can get stuck and cause sores. If your dog has long hair between his toes, especially on the bottom, you may need to trim it even with his pads to keep it clean and give him better traction on smooth surfaces.

Your terrier's nails should be trimmed short. Nails that are allowed to grow so long that they hit the ground will push the toes out of their normal position, distorting the foot and potentially causing lameness and permanent deformity. If your dog sounds like he's tap dancing on hard surfaces, it's time for a trim.

You can do a few things to make nail trimming easier on you and your dog. If the only time you touch your dog's feet is when you want to clip his nails, he'll probably object, so take a little time to teach him that having his feet handled isn't a big deal. When you're relaxing together, hold each of your pup's feet one at a time, gently massaging and flexing his toes. Start with short sessions. If he objects, hold one foot gently and give him a treat *while still holding his foot.* Don't give him a treat after you release his foot—the idea is to reward him for letting you hold it. Don't try to trim his nails until he's comfortable with having his feet held. When he is, try trimming one nail. If he doesn't fight you, go ahead and trim as many nails as you can without resistance. If your dog isn't sure about this, trim one nail, and give him a treat while you're still holding his foot, then quit. Do another nail later. Be sure to continue paw-holding sessions without trimming, too. You'll soon be trimming all his nails in one session without frightening or fighting your dog.

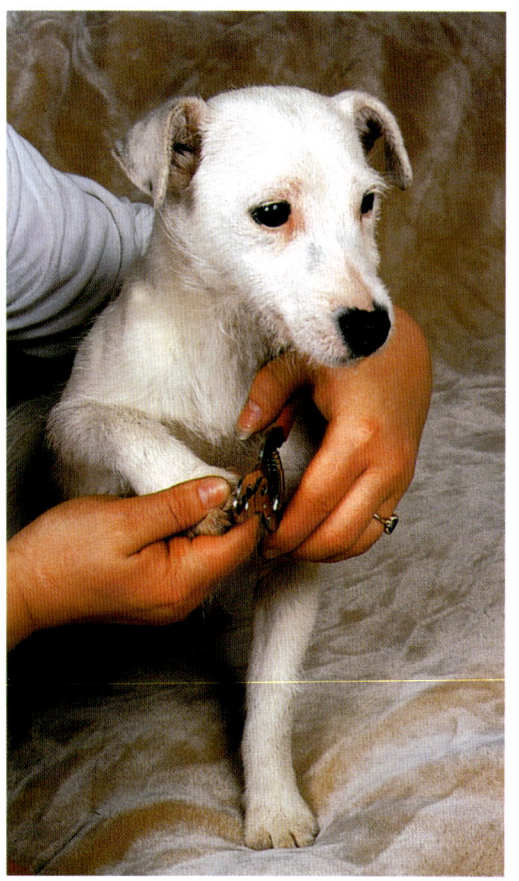

Trim your terrier's nails to keep them from growing too long and distorting the foot.

Before you trim nails, be sure you're prepared. Find a comfortable position and be sure you have sufficient light. If your dog will lie quietly on your lap, that's fine, or you can have him stand, sit, or lie on a grooming table or on a table at a height that's comfortable for you. Be sure the surface he stands on provides traction; spread a rubber mat or towel on it if necessary. Hold your dog's paw gently but firmly, and press gently on the bottom of the foot pad to extend the nail, and trim to just outside the quick, which is the living part of the nail containing blood vessels and nerves. If your dog has light-coloured nails, the quick will look pink. If his nails are dark, cut below the spot where the nail narrows and curves downward. Trim the tip, and then look at the end of the nail. If you see a black dot near the centre of the nail, you're at the quick and it's time to stop trimming. If not, you can shave a little more off. Don't forget to trim your dog's dewclaws, which are located on the insides of the legs above the front feet. Neglected dewclaws can grow around and actually puncture the flesh of the leg.

If you accidentally cut into the quick and cause it to bleed, don't panic. To stop the bleeding, put a little styptic powder (available from pet shops or chemists) or cornflour into the palm of your hand or a shallow dish and dip the nail into it. The powder will stick to the nail and seal the blood vessel. Clippers leave sharp, rough edges, but you can smooth them out with a few short, downward strokes of an emery board. (The ones made for acrylic nails work well on doggy nails.) You can also use a nail grinder to trim and smooth your dog's nails, but before you do, have a groomer or your vet show you the proper technique.

Never push anything, including cotton buds, into your dog's ear canals.

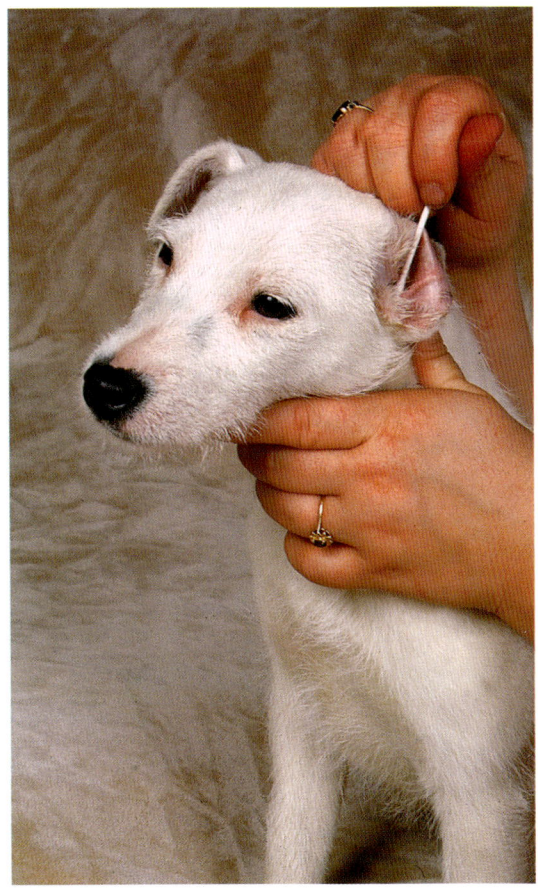

Dull or poorly aligned nail clippers won't cut cleanly and may pinch, which won't make your dog like nail trimming time any better, so be sure your nail clippers are sharp and working well. If you're still not sure how to trim the nails, ask your vet or a groomer to show you how. As a last resort, you can have them done at the vet's surgery or by a groomer, but please don't wait for your dog's annual check-up to get his nails trimmed. They should be done every 3 to 6 weeks, depending on your individual dog.

HOW'S YOUR HEARING?

Ear infections aren't as common in Parson and Jack Russell Terriers are they are in some dog breeds, but they do occur. Allergies, hormonal problems, and excess moisture all can promote abnormal growth of yeast or bacteria in the moist, warm ear

Homemade Ear-Cleaning Solutions

Ear-cleaning products are available from your vet and from pet shops, but they tend to be pricey. You can save money by making your own ear cleaner. Just remember, though, that cleaning solutions will not treat an existing infection. If you think your dog has an ear infection, take him to your vet.

Here are two homemade cleaners that will help make your dog's ears inhospitable to bacteria and yeast. The alcohol also will help dry any moisture in the ear but can be irritating for some dogs. Vinegar helps to control yeast growth in the ear. Use only one of these at a time, not both. And remember to stand back when your dog starts to shake!

Cleaning Solution 1: Mix one part rubbing alcohol and one part white vinegar. Shake well. Use generously to flush the ear once a month or more often if necessary.

Cleaning Solution 2: Mix 2 tablespoons (29.6 ml) of boric acid, 4 ounces (118.3 ml) of rubbing alcohol, and 1 tablespoon (14.8 ml) of glycerine. Shake well. Apply with an eye dropper—one dropper-full in each ear. Press the ear leather to the opening of the ear and massage for a few seconds.

canal, leading to pain, irritation, and foul odours. Ear mites aren't found as often in dogs as they are in cats, but if your dog has mites and is sensitive to mite saliva, he may scratch until he causes serious damage to his tender ears. An active terrier who plays outdoors can also get dirt, plant matter, or other things in his ear, causing irritation and possibly injury or infection.

At least once a week, check your dog's ears by looking at and sniffing them. The skin inside the ear should be pink or flesh coloured, not red or inflamed. A little wax may be present, but it shouldn't be excessive. Dirty looking discharge or a strong or nasty odour is a sign of trouble. Even if you can't see or smell anything unusual, if your dog persistently scratches or rubs at his ears or head, shakes or tilts his head, or cries or pulls away when you touch his ears or the area around them, he needs medical attention. Don't try to treat ear problems with home remedies. Ear infections are painful, and your dog can suffer permanent hearing loss if left untreated. Accurate diagnosis is essential for effective treatment, and using an inappropriate over-the-counter or homemade remedy will prolong your dog's discomfort and could cause more damage, making the infection harder to treat later.

If your dog's ears are not inflamed or sensitive but look a little dirty, you can clean them with a commercial or homemade ear cleaner. Do this outdoors or in a bathroom or other place you can clean easily, because ear cleaning can be messy. To clean the ear, squirt plenty of cleaner into the ear to flush it out, then lay the ear flap over the opening of the ear and massage for a few seconds to work the cleaner into the ear canal. Then, let go and stand back—your dog will shake his head to clear his ear, and cleaner and whatever it flushes will be flung far and wide. Repeat the process with the other ear. When both ears are cleaned, gently wipe them out with a cotton-wool ball or tissue. Never push anything, including cotton buds, into your dog's ear canals. How often you need to clean your dog's ear will depend on your dog. If he has very waxy ears, or if he plays in water frequently, clean his ears about once a week to keep them healthy. If his ears stay nice and clean on their own, you don't need to do anything except check them regularly.

HEALTHY EYES

Russells have intelligent, bright, very appealing eyes. When healthy, they are clear and moist, often with a devilish twinkle to boot. Any sign of redness, swelling, excess tearing, mucous, or squinting can indicate infection, abrasion, or another problem that needs veterinary attention.

You can take some steps to protect your dog's eyes and help keep them healthy. Some mucus at the inner corners of the eyes from time to time is normal. However, if "eye gunk" is excessive or is allowed to build up, it can harbour bacteria that may cause an eye infection. An occasional gentle clean-up with a moist washcloth or tissue, though, will keep your dog's face clean and his eyes healthier. You can also protect your dog's eyes from injury by using good sense when you take him in your vehicle. Nothing evokes the freedom of the open road more than a dog with his head out the window, ears flying in the wind. Unfortunately, freedom comes at a cost, even for dogs. A tiny bit of debris or an insect slamming into an eye at the speed of a moving vehicle can cause serious injury. To prevent this from happening, keep your dog away from open windows, or better yet, have him travel safely in a crate. Similarly, soap and chemicals can cause serious eye damage, including blindness, so be careful when bathing your dog or applying any products on his face.

Tear Stains

If your dog has white hair around his eyes, it may become stained by proteins found in the tears that keep the surface of the eye clean. The stains won't hurt your dog, but they aren't terribly attractive, so you might want to consider using one of the special stain removers made for use around the eyes. Ask your breeder, rescue representative, vet, or a groomer to recommend an effective product.

As your dog ages, his eyes may take on some cloudiness. Most often, this is caused by a change in the lens associated with normal aging, and unless it's severe, it usually has little effect on vision. However, in some cases cloudiness may indicate a cataract, which can affect vision. If you see changes in your dog's eyes, talk to your veterinary surgeon.

As we'll learn in Chapter 8, Parson and Jack Russell Terriers are susceptible to several inherited eye problems, so you might consider having your dog's eyes examined every one to three years by a veterinary ophthalmologist. Your vet can give you a referral. On an individual level, early diagnosis of a problem may be important for effective treatment, or at least to let you plan for your dog's future. Check-ups also are important to the future of the Parson and Jack Russell Terriers as breeds and to your dog's breeder and owners of your dog's relatives, so send copies of the results to your dog's breeder. Responsible breeders want to know their pups' health status.

When healthy, your Russell's eyes should be clear and moist.

Retained Teeth

Puppies, like human babies, are born toothless. Their deciduous, or baby, teeth begin to come in at about four weeks and are replaced by permanent teeth when the puppy is between three and five months old. Once in a while, the permanent tooth fails to push a baby tooth out. Such retained deciduous teeth, most often the incisors or upper canines ("fangs"), will cause the permanent teeth to be misaligned and will keep the jaw bones from developing properly, leading to pain, difficulty eating, and other problems. If you suspect that your pup has retained a baby tooth, take him to your vet. If you have a puppy, check his mouth and teeth every few days.

KEEPING THOSE PEARLY WHITES HEALTHY

Cavities are rare in dogs who eat normal canine diets (no sugary treats!), but gum disease is very common in adult dogs and contributes to a number of other problems. Bacteria and food particles collect along the gum line and form plaque, which will turn to tartar (calculus) and irritate the gums, leading to gingivitis (inflammation of the gum). If tartar builds up under the gums, it causes periodontal disease, resulting in abscesses, infection, and loss of teeth and bone. Unhealthy teeth and gums are the main cause of "dog breath." Less obvious but more serious are the ways in which such bacteria can contribute to heart, liver, and kidney disease when transported by the blood to those organs.

Inspect your dog's mouth frequently to check for signs of injury or disease.

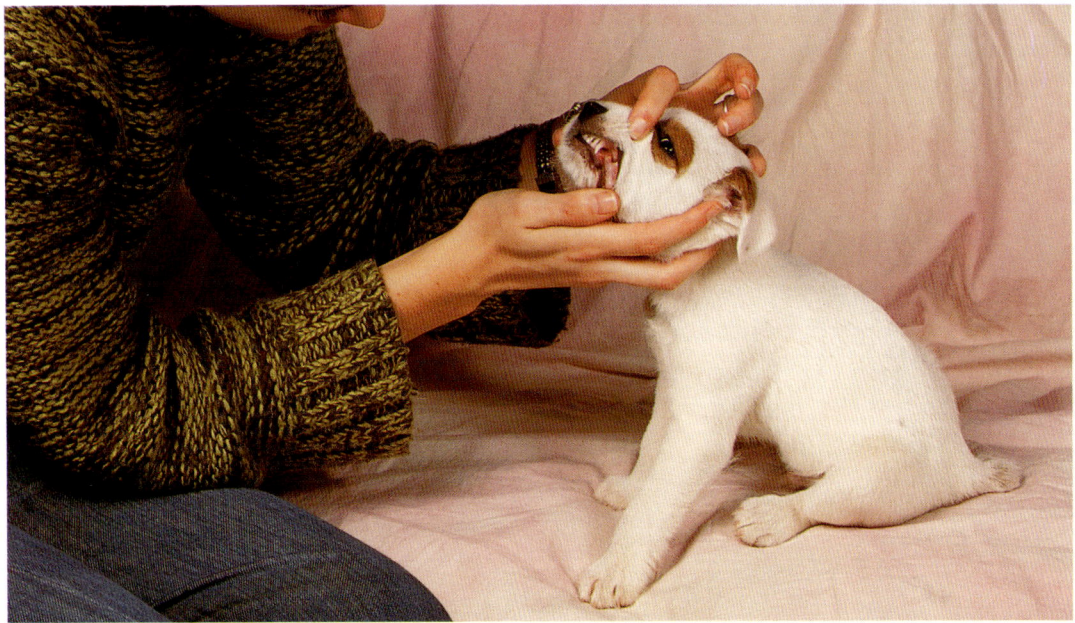

Doggy Toothpaste

Don't use toothpaste made for people on your dog— he won't spit and rinse like humans do, and if he swallows it, he may get sick. Liver toothpaste may not appeal to you, but your dog will like it, and it's much better for him.

Regular doggy dental care may sound like a daunting task, but it's really no harder to care for your dog's teeth than your own. It's just a matter of training your dog to accept dental care as part of regular grooming and training yourself to stick with the regimen. Ideally, your dog should have his teeth brushed every day to remove the plaque, but even every few days will go a long way toward preventing tartar from forming.

Your vet can show you how to brush your dog's teeth properly, and she can recommend toothbrushes, plaque removers, and toothpastes that are safe for use on dogs. Canine toothbrushes are softer and smaller than human toothbrushes, and they are shaped differently. Some people prefer to use a dental sponge—a small, disposable sponge with a flexible handle—for small dogs like Russells. Rubber "finger brushes" also are available for use on dogs. If your dog's gums are sensitive, or if you have difficulty managing his toothbrush, you can wrap surgical gauze around your finger, dampen it with water, dip it in a little canine toothpaste or baking soda, and rub it over your dog's teeth and gums. A diet of high-quality dry dog food also can help slow the formation of plaque, and some companies now offer special foods that are supposed to help prevent plaque. Nylabone chew toys and dental devices, as well as raw or sterilised beef bones, also may help.

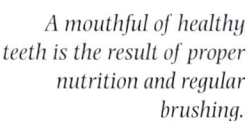

A mouthful of healthy teeth is the result of proper nutrition and regular brushing.

Regular at-home dental care is important, but it isn't enough. Your dog also should have dental check-ups as part of his routine veterinary care. Your vet will check your dog's teeth and mouth, and she will probably recommend thorough cleaning and polishing under anaesthesia once or twice a year. If your pup develops bad breath, visible tartar along the gum line, bleeding gums, or other oral problems between check-ups, take him to your vet. Better to catch a problem early than to let it become a bigger problem.

ANAL SAC CARE

Jokes aside, why do dogs greet one another with mutual rear-end sniffing? Like other predators, your dog has anal sacs (anal glands) that produce an odour that identifies him to other dogs. In a healthy dog, the anal glands, which are located on both sides and slightly below his anus, express, or empty, themselves onto the surface of the stool every time the dog has a bowel movement. The scent deposited there is what makes poop so fascinating to dogs—it tells them who else has passed this way.

Many dogs go their entire lives without ever having a problem, but the anal glands can become impacted if they fail to empty regularly. Impacted glands are not dangerous in themselves, but they are uncomfortable. If your dog has impacted anal glands, he may bite at the area or scoot along the floor, potentially injuring the delicate tissue surrounding his anus. Impacted anal glands also can make defecation difficult or painful, and they can lead to a painful infection or abscess.

Impacted glands often can be relieved by expressing them manually. The odour of anal gland fluid doesn't appeal to people nearly as much as it does to dogs, but if you're brave, you can have your vet or groomer teach you how to express the glands. If that doesn't sound like a skill you want to master, you can have your vet or groomer do the job if and when necessary. Chronically impacted anal glands can be relieved in some cases by feeding the dog a high-fibre diet, causing bulkier stools that express the glands when they pass. The anal glands also can be removed by a vet in serious cases.

Flea Products

Before you use any grooming or flea-prevention product, including a flea collar, on a puppy or on a dog with health problems, read all instructions and warning labels. Better yet, ask your vet. Some products are dangerous for puppies or for dogs with health problems.

HOW TO CHOOSE A PROFESSIONAL GROOMER

Even though your terrier doesn't need a lot of grooming, there still may be times when he needs a clean-up, and you may lack the time or inclination to do it yourself. If you find you need the services of a professional groomer, ask your vet, family, and friends for recommendations. If possible, find a groomer who is especially good with terriers. If you plan to show your dog, be sure that any groomer you go to knows how to groom a Parson or Jack Russell Terrier for the show ring. (Better yet, have your dog's breeder help you learn to do it yourself.)

Most groomers are kind and gentle with dogs and keep clean,

Foxed!

A bold terrier who lives in fox country is likely to have a close encounter of the stinky kind sometime in his life. Here's a popular defoxing formula:

- 1 quart (946 ml) of 3% hydrogen peroxide
- 1/4 cup (59.1 ml) of baking soda
- 1 teaspoon (4.9 ml) of liquid soap

Use the mixture immediately, while it's bubbly, and rinse thoroughly. Don't leave the mixture on your dog for more than a few minutes.

safe environments, but as in any business, there are unfortunate exceptions. Before you entrust your dog to a groomer, here are some questions to ask:

- What training and experience do the groomers in the shop have?
- What shampoos and conditioners do they use?
- Do they use a hand-held drier or cage drier to dry the dogs? If a cage drier, how often will they check your dog? Is someone always present when the drier is on the dog?
- Will they clean your dog's ears?
- Will they check, and if necessary, express the anal glands?
- Will they use sedatives if your dog is uncooperative? If so, are

A puppy who enjoys being handled will also like grooming time.

you comfortable with that idea? If you are, who will sedate and monitor the pet? What training has that person had in the safe use of sedatives and in first aid? What will she do if something goes wrong?

- How long will your dog need to be there? Where will he be kept when he's not being groomed? Where will he be taken to toilet? Is the area fenced?
- What is the normal fee for a Parson or Jack Russell, and what's included in that fee?

The facilities should be clean and tidy, and dogs who aren't being groomed should be in secure, reasonably comfortable cages or crates with access to drinking water. Equipment, such as scissors, combs, brushes, clippers, and grooming tables, should be disinfected between dogs. If you don't feel comfortable about a groomer, don't leave your dog. Trust your instincts.

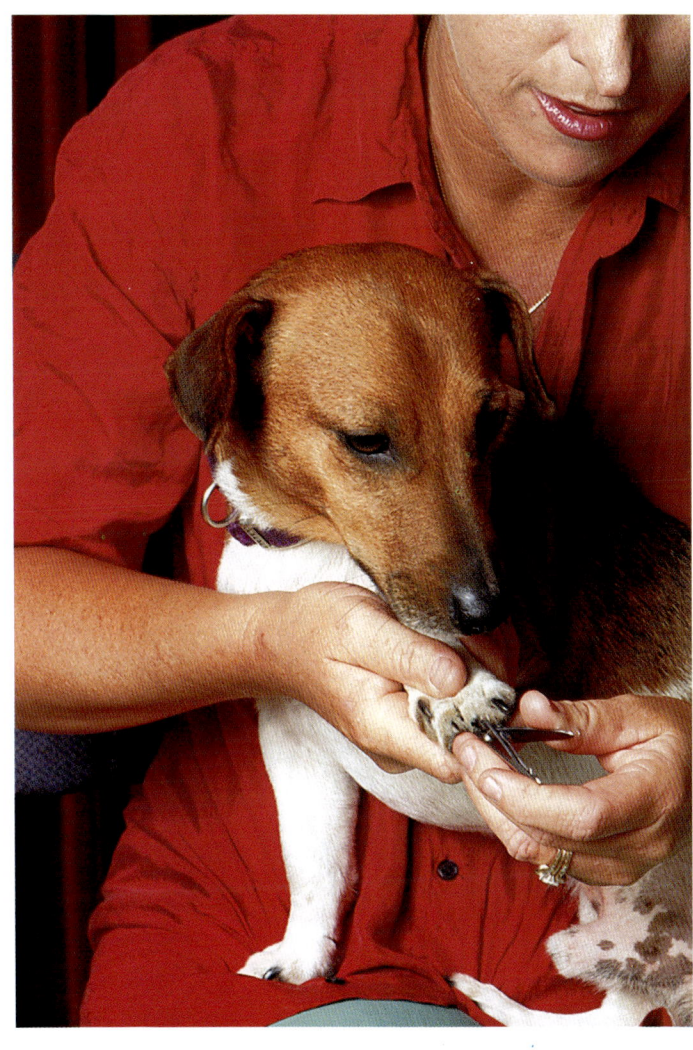

Most groomers are kind and gentle with dogs and maintain clean, safe environments.

Parson and Jack Russells don't need much grooming compared to some other breeds, but regular grooming is still important to your dog's health. Brushing and bathing will keep him clean and allow you to check him for lumps, bumps, nicks, and parasites. Regular dental care will keep his teeth and gums healthy. Regular ear care will prevent infections from setting in, and regular nail trimming will keep his feet healthy. Don't think of grooming as work—think of it as a chance to spend special moments with your dog, strengthening the bond between you.

TRAINING AND BEHAVIOUR

of Your Parson or Jack Russell Terrier

E arlier in this book, we explored your Parson or Jack Russell's heritage as a working terrier. Keeping that information in mind will help you as you train your terrier, because the traits for which his ancestors were originally valued— confidence, tenacity, courage, independence, and intelligence—affect your dog's behaviour and his response to training.

Terriers can certainly be trained, but you have to motivate them to learn and to follow direction. Your terrier will get bored easily, so you need to make training interesting and fun and show him what's in it for him. All training should be done with kindness and respect for your dog, and your dog must also learn to respect you as his leader.

This chapter will look at some basic principles of effective dog training, explore some specific training possibilities for your pup, and outline some problem behaviours your terrier might experience, as well as some effective ways to deal with them.

BEFORE YOU TRAIN

People have a tendency to think of their beloved dogs as "fur people" who have the same kinds of desires and attitudes that humans have, despite their physical differences. But we do our dogs—and ourselves—a great disservice when we fail to see them as the endlessly fascinating creatures that they really are. Our two species have lived side by side, helping and using one another for thousands of years, a remarkable feat for creatures with very different ways of perceiving the world. Ignoring the differences in the ways our two species interact with the world won't enhance your relationship with your dog and may actually damage it.

Instinct or learning is at the root of almost everything your terrier does. (Behaviours that are the exceptions may be caused by outside influences such as illness, injury, or chemicals.) The most effective way to direct your dog's behaviour and to prevent and deal with behavioural problems, then, is to learn about normal canine behaviour and instincts and use that knowledge to your advantage. You can teach your dog what you want and don't want from him if you understand what motivates him and if you plan ahead and invest some time in helping him learn. You can also prevent many potential problem behaviours and put an end to others. Your dog is always learning about you, and he uses what he learns to get what he wants. There's no reason you can't do the same thing.

Why Train Your Terrier?

You may have heard that Parson and Jack Russell Terriers are hard to train, but you've also heard that they're smart. What's going on here? How can a smart dog be difficult to train?

Motivation, not intelligence, makes a dog trainable, or more precisely, makes him willing to be trained. Your terrier's ancestors were developed to work alone, finding and facing an animal that was well armed and fighting for its life. Once he was underground, the dog was on his own and had to work independently and without guidance. He had to be smart, quick, courageous, and determined. Is it any wonder, then, that your terrier is inclined to do things his own way? You should be aware, though, that Parson Russell, the man, also valued his terriers as household companions when they weren't with him hunting fox. Clearly, even Russell's

You can teach your terrier what you want and don't want him to do if you invest some time in helping him learn.

hunting terriers were dogs who could learn to behave themselves in polite company, as can their descendants today.

Training is the process through which your dog develops new habits. Whether you're intentionally training him or not, your terrier is always learning. If he finds that something he tries is either enjoyable or gets him what he wants a time or two, he'll keep doing it. It's your job to anticipate behaviours you don't want from him and to keep him from starting or repeating them. More importantly, you need to teach him the behaviours you do want or find acceptable. Unfortunately, many people focus on "bad dog" behaviours and forget to teach and reward "good dog" behaviours. Try to remove "no!" from your dog-training vocabulary, and when you see your dog doing something he shouldn't do, guide him quickly to a better behaviour. Habits are very hard to change once they're established, so help your dog learn good ones.

Generously reward your terrier with a treat or favourite game when he correctly responds to a command.

Many people think that an intelligent dog like a Parson or Jack Russell will be easier to live with than a less intellectually well-endowed canine. But unless you find ways to stimulate your terrier's mind as well as his body, you may find the opposite to be true. Your terrier's intelligence and independence will probably make him a more challenging dog to train than some because he's easily bored by repetition, and he wants to know what's in it for him. On the other hand, if you do your part, training him creatively and consistently with positive motivational training methods, and if you provide activities that make him think, training your terrier can be rewarding for both of you.

Seven Secrets of Success

There are many reasons to train a dog, and there are many methods of training, but no matter why or how you train, there are

If your dog tends to ignore you, think about how to better get his attention.

seven training principles that always apply. There are times when it's really hard to stick with them, but if you can do so most of the time, these principles will help make your efforts more productive:

1. **Be consistent.** Remember, your dog is not a native speaker of human language. He can learn what "sit" means without much trouble, but, "Aww, sweetie, sit here by me" or "You better sit down right now!" or "Sit...sitsitsit...I said sit!" will be so much noise. Each behaviour should be cued by one command, and each command should mean only one thing. Don't say, "Down" to mean lie down one time and don't jump on me the next. Use different words for different actions.

2. **Be efficient.** If you repeat a command, your dog will quickly learn that he doesn't have to respond until you say, "Come...come....come....come" or yell, "YOU BETTER COME RIGHT NOW!" or put your fists on your hips and glare or otherwise indicate that now you really mean "come." Give a command only once.

3. **Be generous.** While it may be obvious to you why your dog should come when you call him, it may not be so obvious to your dog. Sniffing those tantalising smells in the garden and chasing squirrels are inherently rewarding behaviours, so you need to teach your terrier that coming when you call isn't just required, it's also pleasurable for him. Reward your dog for responding correctly.

4. **Be smart.** If you want your dog to come when you call him, don't try to call your dog in from the garden when you're dripping wet and wrapped in a towel unless you're willing to go and get him anyway. If you repeatedly give commands that your dog doesn't yet understand or that you can't be sure he'll obey without a little help, you will teach him to ignore you. So while your dog is learning a command, don't use that command if you can't make him do it.

5. **Be prepared.** If you will need a training tool to reinforce a command, have it handy. For instance, if your dog doesn't yet

come every time you call him, don't send him out to relieve himself without fastening a long line to his collar so you can reel him in. Keep the long line by the door so that it's there when you need it.

6. **Be cheerful**. Your and your dog are partners, not rivals. Dogs like to hear happy voices, so try to sound happy when you give commands and when you praise. Your dog may not understand all the words, but he'll certainly understand your tone of voice.

7. **Be humane.** Never, ever hit your dog. Hitting doesn't teach your dog what you want him to do, but it does teach him that you can't be trusted. Not only that, but violence begets violence, and many terriers react defensively to being hit.

Setting Goals

It's very hard to reach a goal if you don't know what that goal is. Whether you want a well-behaved pet or a successful canine competitor, you need to decide what it is you want him to know and do. Will you be content if he simply learns to toilet outdoors, walk nicely on lead, and not jump up on your friends? Or do you want to participate in competition, dog-assisted therapy, or other activities with your terrier? Your goals, both long- and short-term, will affect how you go about training your dog.

Spend quality time with your dog to forge a bond of trust, mutual respect, and understanding between the two of you.

Your dog will be learning all the time, so no matter what your goals are, try to get all human members of your household to follow the same rules and use the same words and methods for teaching and reinforcing behaviours. If you're trying to train your dog to stay off the sofa and

A trained dog is a happier companion.

your significant other invites him up, your dog won't know what's acceptable. People are generally a lot harder to train than dogs, but do your best to provide a consistent environment.

A Positive Approach to Training

Ideally, training should not only teach your dog to behave himself, but also help a bond of trust, mutual respect, and understanding develop between you and your dog. Learning and teaching are hard work, but if you also make them lots of fun, you and your terrier will enjoy each other more, and training will progress more quickly. Training through positive reinforcement is fair, fun, and effective.

Positive reinforcement involves rewarding your dog with something he likes for performing a behaviour that you like. Food is highly motivating for many dogs, but so are toys, strokes, and a chance to "kill" a fuzzy toy. To use positive reinforcement effectively, you need to find out what motivates your dog and then use those reinforcers in your training. Enlightened dog trainers do not bully their dogs through heavy-handed punishment—why would anyone do that to a friend?

Some people prefer to use only positive reinforcement in dog training, with no corrections for unwanted behaviours. Other people use a combination of positive reinforcement for correct behaviours and fair, gentle corrections (but no hitting or yelling) for unwanted behaviours. A good obedience instructor and a number of excellent books and websites that focus on training can help you find the approach that works best for you and your dog.

Training Tools

The right equipment will make training your dog easier and more effective, but how do you know what's best? Several different kinds of collars and leads are available, and they all serve different purposes. In the final analysis, the best equipment is whatever works best for you and your dog at a given time. Let's look at some of the options.

Collar

Your dog needs at least one collar, probably two. Your choice of collar will depend on your dog's age, personality, level of training, and the type of training you're doing.

A *flat colla*r may be leather, nylon, or fabric, with a buckle or a quick-release fastener. Your dog should have one flat collar with his name, and your contact details on a tag. If you train with a flat collar, it shouldn't have a tag attached, so you'll need an extra. A flat collar doesn't provide much control, and some dogs learn to slip out of them, but for some dogs and some types of training, a flat collar is a good choice, and it's the only collar that should be used on a young puppy's delicate neck. When a flat collar fits correctly, you should be able to slide two fingers between the fastened collar and your dog's neck.

Your dog should wear a collar during training sessions.

A *martingale collar* is like a flat collar without a fastener. To put it on, you slide it over your dog's head. When your lead pulls against it, the collar will tighten so your dog can't slip out, but it can tighten only so far, so it can't choke him. This is a good choice for a dog who has learned to slip out of a flat collar.

Choke or *slip collars* may be made of metal links, nylon, or leather. An experienced dog trainer can use a choke chain without hurting the dog, but these collars are often misused, making them ineffective for training and control and potentially dangerous to the dog's neck and throat.

A *halter* (or head collar) resembles a horse halter with straps behind the ears and around the muzzle. It controls the dog very effectively by controlling his head. In fact, halters are so effective that many people rely on them for control and never really train their dogs, so that when the halter is off, the dog is disobedient. Another problem with the halter on a small dog is that a quick jerk can twist the dog's head and cause serious injury to the cervical vertebrae.

Lead

You will also need at least one lead. Leather leads are most popular with experienced trainers because they are easy on the hands and give you and your dog a good feel for one another's movements. For a Parson or Jack Russell, you will probably want a 4- (1.2 m) to 6-foot (1.8 m) long lead a quarter (0.6 cm) to half an inch (1.3 cm) wide.

You will need at least one lead before you begin training your terrier.

Treats and Toys

To reinforce your dog for behaviours you want, you will need treats and toys. Be sure to choose things your dog likes—if your dog isn't thrilled with the reward, it's not very rewarding!

Voice, Body, and Attitude

Although the external tools (collars, leads, and treats) are important, you already have some essential dog training tools—your voice, your body, and your attitude. Dogs are keen observers of pitch, tone of voice, and body language, and if you in turn observe your dog carefully, you'll see that he responds to your behaviour and mood. He'll respond better to a happy, high-pitched voice than to shouts, grumbles, and growls, so pay attention to the tone of your commands, praise, and corrections. Try to be relaxed when you train, too; a tense trainer makes for a tense dog. Try to think of training as play and then turn training sessions into games. You'll both enjoy the process a lot more, and your dog will learn more quickly if he's having fun.

You will teach your dog specific words as you train him, but two that are especially important are often neglected by novice trainers: the praise word and the release word. Your praise word tells your dog when he's correct. Find a word your dog doesn't hear all the time—if you're always telling your dog he's a "good boy" just for lying on the couch, don't use "good boy" for praise in training. I use "excellent" to praise my dogs. At first, say the praise word as you give your dog his reward (food or play). He'll soon come to value the praise itself, because it's been associated with good things.

All members of the canine family need to learn household rules.

Your release word tells your dog that he's off the hook for the moment; he sat when you told him to, and now he doesn't have to sit. Many people use, "Okay" to release their dogs, but I'd recommend that you use a word your dog doesn't hear all the time so you don't accidentally release him. I use "free!"

GETTING OFF ON THE RIGHT PAW

Your terrier's training should start as soon as you bring him home, because that's when he begins to learn how to behave. Whether he's a puppy or an adult, he needs to learn the rules and routine, and although he's smart, he can't read your mind. Nothing you buy for your dog will mean a thing if you can't live with him, so give him—and yourself—an education.

Establishing Household Rules

Before you bring your new dog home, decide what he will be allowed and expected to do, and be sure that the humans in the household all understand the rules. If you're getting a puppy, think ahead to how you want him to behave as an adult. Don't allow a puppy special privileges and then take them away from him later— that's unfair and confusing. If anything, a puppy should gain privileges as he matures, not lose them. So if you don't want your adult terrier jumping onto the couch, don't let him do it as a puppy.

Socialisation is an important process that allows your puppy to meet a variety of people and other dogs.

The same goes for basic good manners. If you don't want your adult dog to jump up on you and other people, don't let him do it when he's a puppy. Bad habits are harder to break than prevent, so encourage only good habits in your new dog.

Plan two or three short training sessions in which you focus on one or two behaviours. Take advantage of opportunities throughout the day to teach and reinforce the behaviours you want in your dog. Puppies have very short attention spans, but they learn very quickly. Thus, frequent, very brief training sessions on basic lessons, like sit, come, and down, will be more productive than occasional long sessions. Older dogs can focus longer, but they're easily bored by repetition. As your dog matures, you can train for longer periods, but don't focus on any one thing for more than a few minutes at a time. If your dog performs the lesson correctly, move on to something else.

The Importance of Socialisation

Socialisation is the process of familiarising your puppy with the world around him. Puppies and adolescent dogs need to meet a wide variety of people—old, young, male, female, and of different races and professions. Puppies also need to meet other non-aggressive dogs and to experience as many sights and sounds as you can provide.

Proper socialisation will make your adult dog more confident and comfortable throughout his life. Socialisation with people is particularly important between the ages of 7 and 14 weeks, but the process should continue throughout puberty and young adulthood.

When your dog is 12 to 18 months old, he may lose some of his manners and flex his muscles a bit, challenging some members of the household for higher rank in the "pack" to which he belongs, including the human members. He is, after all, the equivalent of a teenager. Patience and firm, consistent reinforcement of household manners and rules will help the human members of your household keep their socially superior positions in your dog's eyes. This is an excellent time to take an obedience class or two, even if your dog has already completed one.

Crate Training

Most experienced dog owners consider a crate to be essential for raising and training a puppy or new dog. Used properly, a crate will keep your pup and your belongings safe and preserve your sanity as your puppy develops into a responsible adult. Most dogs quickly accept their crates as their very own dens, and many dogs go into their crates on their own once they're used to them. Your

An open pen can be used to confine your puppy or dog so that he can't get into mischief.

dog's crate should be just big enough to let him stand up, turn around, and lie down—about 16 inches (40.6 cm) wide by 20 inches (50.8 cm) deep.

If he hasn't been crated before, your dog may whine, bark, howl, and otherwise raise a ruckus when learning about his crate. Don't give in! If you let him out when he's noisy, he'll quickly learn that all he has to do to be let loose is to make annoying noises. Wait until he is quiet— and he eventually will be—and then reward him either with a treat in the crate or by letting him out. Don't let him out and then give him a treat, or he'll think you're rewarding him for getting out of the crate.

Crates and Housetraining

If you're housetraining a puppy, a crate used properly will speed up the process. A healthy dog raised in clean surroundings won't want to sleep where he messes, and making it harder for your pup to toilet at one end of the crate and lie down at the other end will make housetraining easier. You can do this by using a smaller crate than your dog will need as an adult or by blocking off part of an adult-sized crate to limit the usable space. Also, many puppies like to rip things up, and padding soaks up urine and makes it less offensive to a pup, so you might want to forget about bedding in the crate until your puppy is housetrained and past the bedding shredding stage. If you do use bedding, be sure to keep it clean, and don't use newspaper or pads (which are impregnated with chemicals that tell the puppy "toilet here").

Used properly, a crate will keep your dog and your belongings safe.

Crates and Punishment

A crate should never be used for punishment. Remember, it should be a safe, desirable place for your dog. However, a crate is a good, safe place for a time-out if your pup (or you) needs one. Tired puppies, like tired children, often become cranky and a bit hyperactive and need to be put to bed for a nap. To avoid making it seem like punishment, don't shove your pup into his crate forcibly. Instead, toss a toy or treat in and say, "Crate" or "Kennel." Soon, you'll be able to give him the command and reward him after he gets into the crate. Praise him, give him a treat or special toy that he gets only when crated, and quietly close the door. Your dog's crate will be more attractive to him if you feed him there, at least for a while. If possible, keep the crate near where you are, and have your pup sleep in his crate in your bedroom at night, so that it won't seem like an isolation cell to him.

Paper Training

Should you train your pup to relieve himself on newspaper in the house? I'm not a fan of paper training. If you want your dog to toilet outdoors as an adult, why train him to go indoors — even on papers — as a pup? However, if you work long hours and no one can let the dog out, paper training may be a viable option.

Overusing the Crate

Crates should not, of course, be overused. The general rule for a puppy is to crate him his age in months plus one. So if your puppy is six months old, don't crate him longer than seven hours. Older dogs can usually last at least seven or eight hours or may not need to be crated in your absence, although that depends on your circumstances. These are just rough guidelines, of course. Your three-month-old puppy may be fine for three hours between breaks but wet his crate if you leave him in there for longer than that. It's your responsibility to figure out your pup's limits and to enable him to be successful within those limits.

Does this mean that working people can't have puppies? No, of course not. But it does mean that if you have to be gone all day, you need to plan ahead before you bring your puppy home. It's unrealistic and unfair to ask a puppy to spend eight or nine hours alone, and worse to expect him not to toilet for that long or to lie in filth until you get home. You won't enjoy the cleanup, either. If no one in your family is available to give your pup a midday break, you could hire a reliable pet sitter or dog walker to come in or perhaps barter services with a reliable friend or neighbour.

Don't turn your dog's time in a crate into solitary confinement. Give him something to do while he's crated. Chewing relieves the pressures of teething for puppies and is a satisfying pastime and stress reliever for older dogs. Just be sure that his toys are safe.

Housetraining

Housetraining is at the top of most dog owners' lists of training priorities. If you're careful to take your puppy out when he needs to toilet and patient when he has the occasional accident, housetraining should go quickly and smoothly. If you've adopted an adult who hasn't been housetrained, the guidelines that follow apply as well, with the added advantage that your dog will have better control of his bodily functions. If a dog of any age has

If you work long hours and have no other alternatives, paper training may be a viable option for you.

control problems beyond what you think is normal, talk to your vet to rule out physical problems.

The first rule of housetraining is that you need to be patient. Remember, a puppy is a baby. He doesn't have complete control of his bladder or bowels, and by the time he knows he has to go, he may not be able to hold it any longer. It's your job—not your puppy's— to keep him off your new carpet until he's reliable and to teach him where he should toilet and supervise him carefully. Most puppies indicate when they're going to go, so whenever your pup is loose in the house, watch him closely. If he turns in circles, sniffs the floor, or arches his back, *pick him up and take him out.* Don't expect him to walk out the door once he starts to go, because he may not be able to control his bladder or bowels while doing so. Help him to succeed.

Your pup should go outside after every meal, first thing in the morning, last thing at night, as soon as he wakes up, after active play, and when you hear him stirring in the middle of the night. Take him on lead to the place you want him to use, and don't play with him until he's finished. If he doesn't go within 10 minutes, crate him for 10 to 15 minutes and then take him out again. When he relieves himself, reward him with praise and a treat or short playtime. Wait a few minutes before you take him in to be sure he's finished.

Accidents

If your pup has an accident because no one was watching him, it's essential to remove all traces of odour from that spot. Remember, your terrier has a much better nose than you have, and if he smells traces of urine or faeces, he'll think he's found the toilet. You need a special cleanser (available in pet shops), which is designed to eliminate organic odours. For urine odours (but not faeces) you can also use an inexpensive 50-50 mixture of white vinegar and water.

Don't yell at your puppy or punish him for accidents, and *never* rub his nose in them. Such methods are abusive and ineffective. The human in charge is the one who should be scolded for giving your pup the chance to make a mistake. Your dog won't toilet in the house to annoy you. He'll do it because he has to go and hasn't yet learned how to tell you to open the door. You can yell until you're hoarse, and your pup still won't understand why you're upset about urine on the new carpet.

Housetraining Tips

Here are a few other tips that will help with housetraining:

- If you buy a puppy, buy from a responsible breeder who keeps her puppies in a clean environment. Puppies who spend their first weeks in filth are notoriously difficult to housetrain.
- Feed high-quality dry dog food. Your dog's stools will be smaller and more compact, and he'll have better control of his bowels.
- Feed your pup on a regular schedule until he's reliably housetrained.

Be cautious about asking your puppy to engage in strenuous activities until his bones and joints mature.

Why Go to Doggy School?

You're actually training your dog all the time that you're with him, so he gets most of his training at home or out and about. To train effectively, though, you need to learn how to communicate well with your dog. Good training books and articles will certainly help, but nothing replaces the benefits of learning from a qualified instructor. A good obedience class teaches you to train your dog and gives your pup a chance to socialise with people and other dogs. The community and support of other people who also love dogs is a special bonus.

A good puppy class will help you get your puppy's training started and will promote good canine social skills. Puppy classes usually meet once a week for four to eight weeks, and you'll be expected to work with your puppy every day. Even very young puppies can learn basic commands like sit, down, come, and stay for short periods, as well as skills that will be used in more advanced training later. Don't expect your puppy to perform perfectly, and keep training fun! For an older puppy or dog, or a pup who has successfully completed a puppy class, a basic obedience class that teaches manners and promotes social skills is your best bet.

If you plan eventually to participate in canine sports, look for an instructor who understands your goals. Early training should provide a sound foundation for more advanced training, and your instructor should help you and your dog avoid learning habits that you will later have to unlearn. Be cautious about asking your pup to perform strenuous activities — jumping, weaving through poles, and similar things — until his bones and joints mature. In the meantime, there's no reason he can't learn to pay attention, follow directions, and obey basic commands.

Despite the occasional ad for quick routes to a fully trained dog, there are no shortcuts. Some training methods are more effective than others with certain dogs, and some dogs and people are quicker than others to learn certain skills, but no dog or dog owner is fully trained in six or eight weeks. The goal of obedience training should be to create a partnership built on two-way communication and respect between you and your dog. Intimidation and abuse have no place in dog training, so look for an instructor who uses positive, motivational training methods. You and your dog will both be happier in the long run.

- While you're housetraining your pup, don't feed him within four hours of bedtime, and remove his water two hours before bedtime.
- Limit your dog to a room with a responsible, observant person present until he's reliably housetrained.
- Keep your canine toilet area clean and free of faeces. Your dog doesn't want to step in it any more than you do.

Your puppy may take several months to be fully reliable, partly because he won't have complete physical control of his bladder and bowels until he grows a bit. If you don't have the time or patience to housetrain a puppy, an older puppy or adult who is already trained is a better choice for you. Frequent accidents in the house at six months or older may indicate a medical problem, so if that's the case, talk to your veterinary surgeon.

Lead Training

You should be able to walk your dog without having your arm pulled out of its socket or your legs trapped in a wrap-around lead, so begin lead training your dog as soon as you bring him home. Proper equipment will go a long way towards having a dog who behaves on lead. Be sure your dog's collar is appropriate to your needs and fits him properly, and that your lead is long enough to allow your dog reasonable freedom of movement but not so long that it's hard for you to manage.

A pulling dog is no fun to walk. Fortunately, pulling can be stopped. If you're training a puppy, or if your adult terrier is responsive and submissive to you, try the "no forward progress" response first: If your pup pulls, stop and stand still until he stops pulling. If he stops, praise him and continue walking. If he pulls again, halt. Your walks may be short for a few days, but your dog will soon figure out that pulling gets him the opposite of what he wants.

Don't let your dog get into the habit of pulling when you walk him.

If simply stopping doesn't work, change directions so that pulling not only keeps your dog from moving toward the object of his desire but actually makes you—and him—move away from it. Do this calmly, and don't say a word. Grasp your lead and set your hands together in front of your waist so that you don't jerk your dog with your hands. When he starts to pull, turn and walk in a different direction. Don't wait for him, and don't talk to him until he catches up with you. When he does, praise him, and try turning back in the original direction. Give him a treat occasionally when he's moving happily in the direction you want to go, without pulling. Most dogs quickly get the idea.

Some puppies and dogs, though, are just so determined to see what's up ahead that they need more control. If your dog simply isn't responding, you may need a different type of collar (see the discussion of collars earlier in the chapter), and an obedience class (or another one if you've been through one already) would definitely be a good idea.

Teaching Come as a Group Game

You can make a group game of teaching your dog to come to everyone in the household by calling him back and forth from one person to another. Make sure that only one person calls at a time, that everyone uses the same word and says it just once, and that each person rewards the dog for coming.

FIVE COMMANDS EVERY DOG SHOULD KNOW

Your terrier is certainly capable of learning a wide range of behaviours, but if he responds reliably to the five basic commands—come, sit, down, stay, and leave it—you'll find living with him is much more pleasant. There are many ways to teach these behaviours, of course, but I'll tell you how I personally teach them so that you can get started. You should still take your dog through at least one obedience class, and I would suggest you read a variety of training books and articles as well. No single method works for every dog or person, so if one isn't working for you, look for another.

Come

One of the most important things you can teach your dog is to come when you call. Most people want their dogs to come when called for the sake of convenience, and that can certainly be important—nobody wants to chase a disobedient dog around the garden in the dark. But more important, a dog who comes reliably when called is safer than one who doesn't.

To teach come, put your puppy or dog on lead and take him to a very small room or fenced area so that he can't go very far. Have a toy he likes or a small, yummy treat. Say, "Fido, come!" *only once* in a happy, playful voice. Do whatever you have to do other than repeating the command to get your dog to come to you—act silly, walk or run the other way, crouch down, or play with the toy. If he doesn't come on his own, gently pull him in with the lead. If he starts to come on his own after you pull, great—stop pulling. If he doesn't come, gently guide him to you with the lead. When he gets to you, on his own or with a little help, praise and reward him with the treat or a quick game with the toy. Then let him return to whatever he was doing before you called. Repeat the process two or three times, then quit. Do this several times a day if possible.

Sounds simple, doesn't it? Then why do so many pet dogs not come when their people call? Well, the answer is that most people teach their dogs to ignore them by repeating commands over and over again or by giving commands that the dog obeys only part of the time. Let's see how you can make sure you don't teach your dog to ignore you when you call or when you give other commands. (These principles apply to other training, too.)

• Always make obeying your command a pleasant thing for

your dog to do. He should believe that you are the safest, most fun place he could be. Never call your dog to you for something he finds unpleasant, and never ever punish him when he comes to you.

- Always praise your dog for coming when you call, and from time to time reward him as well with something he likes, such as a treat, toy, or belly rub.

- Always use the same word when you call—common commands to call a dog are "come" or "here." The word itself doesn't matter, but don't confuse your dog with inconsistent word choice.

- Never repeat the command, because this simply teaches your dog to ignore you. Say it once. If he doesn't come when you call, get him and put his lead on. Then call him once and pull him in with the lead. Don't forget to praise and reward him for coming! Then, remove the lead and call him to you. If he comes, reward him. If not, repeat the process. Stay calm and upbeat; patience while he's learning will result in a lifetime of reliable recalls.

The sit command can be used to gain control of your dog and give him something to focus on.

- Never let your terrier off lead in an unfenced area if he doesn't come. This means that he should come on the first command every single time he's called, even if there are squirrels or other distractions in the area. That level of reliability is not common! Even if you consider your dog to be reliable, remember that a single lapse in obedience can get your dog killed. Leads save lives.

- Never give a command you can't enforce, especially while your dog is still learning the command. If you can't be sure your dog will come when you call, put him on a lead or long line. If he learns that he must always obey, eventually he won't think of not obeying—most of the time, at least!

Sit

Sit can be used to gain control of your dog and give him something to do

Sidebar: 1-2-3 Sit

Teaching your terrier to sit is one of the easiest things to do if you follow these steps:

1. Entice your dog with a really yummy treat, such as small pieces of sausage or cheese. Let him sniff the food in your hand, but don't give it to him.
2. When you have his full attention, hold the food near his nose, and then slowly move your hand up and over his head toward his tail.
3. As his head follows the treat, his hind legs should bend into a sit. The instant his rear hits the floor, say "Sit," and give him the treat.

You'll be surprised and delighted how quickly he gets the idea. Practice several times a day.

instead of something you don't want him to do, like jumping on you or spinning in circles while you try to put his lead on him. Most dogs seem to learn to sit on cue in certain situations even if they never learn any other command, because people often reward sits with food (or perhaps the dogs train them to do that!). Sitting can be handy at other times, too, so it's a good command to teach even when you aren't offering dinner or treats. If you plan to compete in obedience or agility, a good sit response is essential.

Start with your dog on lead or confined in a small space. Hold a small treat in front of his nose, but don't let him take it—close your fist over it if necessary. When your dog shows interest in the treat, slowly raise it just high enough to pass over his head, and move it slowly toward his tail. As his head comes up to follow the treat, his rear has to go down (unless you lift the treat too high, in which case he'll probably jump for it). When your dog starts to bend his hind legs to sit, say, "Sit" as you continue to move the treat slowly backward. The instant his rear hits the floor, praise and reward him with the treat, and then release him. If he stands up before you release him, don't give the treat, or you'll be rewarding him for getting up, not for sitting. Just have him sit again, and give him the treat before you release him. Repeat three or four times, then quit.

When your dog sits promptly on command, start requiring him to sit for a longer time before you give him the treat, and have him continue to sit after the treat before you release him. Eventually, you can wean away the treat, rewarding him with praise for sitting and with play and praise for the release. Your dog should eventually sit on the first command and stay sitting without another command until you release him.

Down

Teach your dog to lie down on command no matter where he is or what he's doing. Most people teach their dogs to down from a sit, but I like to teach the down from a stand for three reasons. First, a quick response to the down can save his life. Suppose your dog gets loose and is across the street, and a car is coming. Obviously, you don't want him to come to you, but you do want some control. The down is extremely useful in a situation like this. I've also found that frightened or confused dogs are more likely to respond to the down than to come. My other two reasons are less dramatic. Efficiency is one; getting your dog to sit and then lie down requires two commands. Not a big deal usually, but I prefer to get to the behaviour I want with a single command whenever possible. Finally, if you plan to compete in obedience beyond the Novice level, your dog will have to perform a "moving down" in Open and a "signal down" in Utility. It's much easier to teach your dog those manoeuvres if he doesn't think he has to sit in order to lie down. If he's already trained to lie down from a sit, that's fine. If you want to teach him to do it from a stand, consider using a different command. I've heard people use "drop," "crash," and other words.

To teach your dog to down, start with your dog in the standing position. You may want to kneel at first rather than bending over each time. Hold a treat in your hand and slowly move your hand under your dog's chin toward his front legs, lowering it as you go. As his head follows the treat, he should fold himself into a down position. If his rear stays up, gently guide it down. As soon as he's all the way down, praise him and give him the treat. When he's responding to the moving treat by folding quickly backward into a down, add your command, telling him, "Down" (or your other word) as you begin. When he's doing that quickly and reliably, give him the command, but don't move your hand toward him. When he's down, praise and reward. Be sure to give him the treat while he's down, not after he jumps up!

You should teach your dog to lie down on command no matter where he is or what he is doing.

Teaching Stay

Once your dog understands sit and down, you can begin introducing stay. Working from either position, stand close to your dog and say "Stay." If he moves, place him back in position and start again. Have him stay for just a few seconds at first, increasing the time gradually as he gets it. Always release him with an "okay" or another release word of your choosing when he has stayed for the time you want.

Slowly increase the length of time he has to stay down before getting the treat; you don't want him to learn to be a jack-in-the-box. When he's reliable with you standing close to him, start giving the command when he's farther away (add distance very slowly) or moving.

If your pup steps back instead of lying down, move your hand with the treat toward him and down a little faster. You can use very light pressure between his shoulder blades to guide him into the down if necessary. If his rear stays up when his front end is down, press lightly on his hips. If he doesn't go down, don't try to force him. Keep the treat close to the ground with one hand, and cradle his hind legs from behind with the other, gently moving your arm forward around the hind legs until he folds down. Then praise and reward him.

Keep training sessions short—5 to 10 minutes for a puppy and up to 20 minutes or so for an adult. You can have several training sessions throughout the day, and you can also integrate training into your regular routine. For example, have your dog lie down before giving him his dinner or throwing his tennis ball.

Stay

The stay command tells your dog not to move from whatever position he's in until you release him. I teach the stay initially in the down position, because it's the easiest for the dog to hold without moving. If he learns the concept of staying where he is in a down, he'll learn to stay in a sit and a stand more easily.

To teach the stay, first have your dog lie down. When he is completely down, tell him, "Stay." If he starts to get up, put him back in the down position. Don't repeat the command; he needs to learn to remember it and respond on the first command. When he has stayed down a few seconds, praise, reward, and release him, in that order. Start with very short stays—less than a minute—and stand close to your dog. Very slowly increase the time until he will stay five minutes with you standing close to him.

When your dog is reliable for five minutes with you right there, tell him, "Down" and "Stay," and take one step away from him. Have him stay for 30 seconds, then step back, praise, reward, and release. Build the time up slowly to five minutes. Repeat this process as you increase distance, reducing the length of time and building it back up every time you add distance. If your dog starts popping up, fidgeting, or whining before the time is up, stand a little closer for a few days until he's comfortable again with that distance for that length of time. Then proceed to add distance.

Don't forget that you must release your dog before he's allowed to move out of a stay. Don't let him decide for himself when he's finished. Use the stay command only when you will be present to release your dog, not to keep him from running out the door when you're leaving for an evening out!

Practice down-stays in different environments—it's important that your dog learns to stay just as reliably away from home as in the comfort of your living room. Of course, make sure you're always in a position to restrain him if necessary. For example, if you practice in a squirrel-infested park, keep him on a lead or long line. Practice stays while you're doing other things around the house. Just don't forget that you told him to stay—don't let him wander away, and don't forget to come back and release him. If you want your dog to obey commands reliably, you have to give and cancel them reliably, too.

When your dog understands and obeys the stay command when he's lying down, repeat the same process to teach him to sit and stay. Don't cut corners on time and distance, because to your dog, a sit-stay and a down-stay are completely different. Be patient, and keep time and distance short until your dog is really dependable. Establishing a solid foundation at this stage of training will save you a lot of frustration and remedial training later.

Gradually increase the amount of time you ask your dog to stay so that he understands what you want.

Leave It!

The leave it command tells your dog that he's not allowed to touch or chase something that has piqued his interest. It's a useful command in many situations and has saved many a ham sandwich from pilfering canine jaws!

To teach the leave it successfully, you need to make sure that your dog knows two things: first, that obeying you is more rewarding than obtaining the object of his desires, and second, he'll never get the thing he's after. To convey these points, you must reward your dog for leaving whatever he covets with something he considers worthwhile. You must also control the situation so that your dog

The leave it command tells your dog that he's not allowed to touch or chase something that has sparked his interest.

cannot get whatever he's after. If he does, his disobedience is self rewarding. So, as when teaching him to come when called, if you can't enforce the leave it command when you're teaching it, don't use it.

A caution before you begin: If your dog has a tendency to guard food or other resources, don't try to teach the leave it command on your own. Get professional help from an experienced trainer of terriers or a qualified behaviourist. And regardless of your dog's behavioural history, teach children never to take things from a dog, even a dog they know. If the dog has something he shouldn't have, teach the kids to tell an adult.

To teach the leave it command, your dog must be on a lead, because if you can't control the situation, he'll only learn to ignore you. Start by putting something that you know your dog will find interesting on or near the floor. Don't use his regular toys or food, because that just wouldn't be fair to him. Use something he's never seen before or that he's not allowed to have but will probably try to pick up or investigate. Have some wonderful treats ready—maybe something extra special like tiny bits of cheese or meat. Once the lead is on your dog, walk him near the target object, and be sure the lead is short so that you can prevent him from getting it. As soon as he shows interest in the object, say, "Leave it!" and walk quickly away—he'll have to follow you because of the lead. (You can also pull the dog away while you stand still, but I like to keep moving so that the dog refocuses quickly.) As soon as your dog looks at you instead of the object, praise him and give him a treat. Make a big fuss about what a good dog he is. Repeat the process three or four times, then quit. Be sure to remove the object before you remove your dog's lead!

If you perform this exercise a few times a day, your dog should learn to "leave it" quickly, but be aware of potential training hazards. If your dog gets the target object, take it away from him if you can do so safely. Do not try to take anything from your dog if he growls or guards it, because you could get bitten. Get professional help if he displays any of those signs.

Once your dog learns to leave things alone when you tell him, you won't need to reward him with treats. However, always praise him lavishly for obeying this command, and do something fun to make up for his disappointment in not attaining the object of his desire. We all know how hard it is to resist temptation!

GETTING A GRIP ON PROBLEM BEHAVIOURS

With careful planning and quick responses, you can prevent most problem behaviours and eliminate most others fairly easily. The following principles will help you deal with most problems.

First, you need to determine why your dog is doing what he's doing. Is he acting on an instinct? Is he bored and full of energy? Have you inadvertently taught him an obnoxious behaviour that gets the results he wants? Is your terrier training you, instead of the other way around? If he barks at you, do you hop up and hand him a biscuit? If so, you're not alone—lots of smart dogs train their owners! You can redirect the situation by either completely ignoring him (a behaviour that is never rewarded disappears) or by requiring him to do something to earn what he wants.

It's easier to teach your dog to do *something* than to teach him to do *nothing*. If he does something you don't like, give him an acceptable alternative. For example, if he takes your slipper, take it from him and give him a dog toy.

Prevention works wonders, too. If your dog can't be trusted, crate him when you can't watch him. If your terrier digs holes when he's alone in the garden for 20 minutes, don't leave him alone in the

Learning "Leave It"

There will be many times when your dog wants to put something in his mouth that you find objectionable. Remember, your dog is low to the ground; things are much more enticing to him down there! You'll need to train him with a lead on so you can restrain him from reaching the offending object as you say "Leave it." Get his attention with a treat, and give it to him as you praise him for listening. Remove the object, but make sure to replace it with something enjoyable, like another small treat, a toy, or a walk.

If your dog hasn't learned to come when you call, don't let him off lead.

garden for more than 15 minutes. If he hasn't learned to come when you call him, don't let him off lead.

Be sure your terrier gets plenty of physical exercise, too. Remember, his ancestors were developed to have the stamina to hunt all day, so he has lots of energy that needs to be channelled into safe exercise, and you need to help him do that. Very few dogs self exercise, and if yours does, he'll very likely do things you won't like in the process. Your terrier's quick little mind also needs exercise. Some dog toys are designed to provide mental stimulation, like hard plastic cubes that randomly dispense bits of food as the dog rolls them, for example. Advanced training relieves boredom and the behaviour problems it causes, provides physical exercise, and makes for a better companion. Even if you don't work on preventing or solving a specific problem, training your dog makes him more secure and builds his trust in you, and that usually results in better behaviour across the board. Obedience, agility, tricks, and taking part in other sports are fun activities for terriers, and you don't have to compete to reap their benefits.

Digging

Your terrier comes from a long line of diggers bred by people who appreciated their excavation skills, so it should come as no surprise that he likes to dig holes in the ground. Many dogs like to dig, but for a terrier, digging is as natural and necessary as breathing. If he smells or hears evidence of little furry animals under the surface, he'll want to unearth them. If he has a bone or other treasure, he might decide to bury it. If you leave your dog alone in the garden, he might try his paw at landscaping to relieve his boredom, expend his energy, and fulfill his deepest instinctive desire.

A serious digger can quickly remodel a lovely garden into what looks like a prairie dog town, and you almost certainly will want to keep that from happening where you live. You could supervise all of your dog's outdoor time, but that's not a practical solution for most people. Fortunately, you can discourage and redirect inappropriate digging. Some of these methods work with some dogs, but not all, and you're working against your dog's natural instinct. However, if you're at least as smart and determined as your terrier, you can enjoy your dog and a hole-free garden as well.

Solution

It's very difficult, if not impossible, to prevent a dog from behaving as his instincts tell him to. Your terrier wants and even needs to feel the earth move under his feet, so why not give him his own personal recreational digging spot? Pick a place with loose sand or sandy soil, which is cleaner than clay or loam and a lot more fun to send flying. Build your dog a sandbox if necessary, making sure the sand is deep enough that he can really dig in. (You should also make sure that you have a barrier to control the flying sand or dirt.) Bury a toy or treat, bring your pup to the spot, and let him sniff. Encourage him to dig, praise him when he does, and encourage him to find the buried treasure. Repeat the process over a few days. In the meantime, if you see your dog digging in a different part of the garden, say, "Leave it," and take him to his legal spot. Don't leave him alone in the garden until you're confident that he won't dig where you don't want him to.

If your dog still insists on digging in one special place where you don't want a pit, try filling or covering his hole with rocks, a pot, or some other dig-proof barrier. You can also bury chicken wire under the top layer of soil in a garden; plants will still be able to grow, but your dog's digging will be curtailed. If your dog is prone to tunnelling under fences, block him by burying the fencing a few inches into the soil, or bury chicken wire horizontally or vertically where he digs. Check the fence line frequently, too, to be sure he hasn't dug himself an escape route.

For a terrier, digging is a natural instinct that may need to be redirected to a more appropriate location.

Be careful about what you use in your garden that might encourage your dog to dig. Soil supplements such as bonemeal and blood meal, for instance, smell like animal parts (which they are) and reek of buried treasure to your terrier.

You'll find a number of products on the market

Keeping Toys Interesting

Ever notice how much fun it is to find something you had hidden away for a while? Same goes for your dog. If all his toys are available all the time, they get to be kind of boring. But if you give him two or three toys at a time—something hard to chew on, something he can roll and chase, and something soft that he can shake and "kill"—and switch them with other toys every few days, they'll be much more enticing.

that supposedly discourage diggers, but many of them don't work all that well, and some are dangerous. Home remedies like black and cayenne pepper sprinkled on top of the soil stop some dogs; others seem to like peppery soil. Many people use mothballs to repel animals, but they are highly toxic. Aside from their ineffectiveness and possible risks to your dog, such products don't get to the root of the behaviour. They may keep your dog from digging in some areas, but they don't offer him any alternative behaviour to use up the energy and drive that made him dig to begin with. You can be sure that a clever terrier will find another hobby, and you probably won't like it any better than you liked his digging. A better approach is to channel your terrier's energy and instinct into something you and your dog can both accept. Practicing basic obedience skills, playing games like hide-and-seek or retrieve the toy, and learning cute tricks will help and be fun for both of you. More advanced training in obedience, agility, and other sports is even better, whether you intend to compete or not.

Chewing

Smart though he may be, your dog can't read a good book or play computer games to pass the time or relieve stress. He can, however, have a good chew on a nice raw knuckle bone or safe, hard chew toy. Gnawing serves several purposes: It dispels boredom, eases the discomfort of teething, and is highly enjoyable. Chewing is a natural activity for a dog, and it has the potential to become a problem only because your dog wasn't born knowing what he may and may not chew. Chair leg or stick, shoe or leather chewy—what's the difference? It's your responsibility to help your dog learn that there is a difference and to prevent him from making mistakes. Chewing the wrong things will undoubtedly make you unhappy and can be dangerous for your dog.

Although many dogs enjoy a good chew well into old age, puppies and adolescent dogs are the serious chewers in dogdom. Your puppy's deciduous (baby) teeth started to come in when he was about four weeks old. When he's four to five months old, his deciduous teeth will loosen, fall out, and be replaced by permanent (adult) teeth. During this teething (or reteething) process, your pup's gums will be swollen, and he'll have some discomfort. Chewing provides relief.

Solution

As always, prevention is the ideal treatment for chewing. Begin by putting anything you don't want your dog to chew out of his reach. Don't underestimate a terrier's ability to get things from high places and other "safe" locations. Locked away out of sight is safest, and if the objects are hazardous to your dog's health and safety, locking them up is a critical safety measure.

Training is also important. Teach your dog that some things are his to chew, but not all things. If he picks up something he shouldn't have, gently take it from him and replace it with one of his toys. Don't yell, hit, or punish him—that won't teach him what's right, and it may provoke other problem behaviours. Think about what you give him to chew, too. If you give him old shoes or socks to play with, for example, how can you be surprised when he chews your new ones? If your dog likes to chew and rip things up, don't ever leave him unsupervised where he can get things he shouldn't have. Confine your dog to his crate with a nice Nylabone chew toy or large, raw bone to play with when you can't watch him. Be consistent and vigilant, and your terrier will learn what he is and isn't allowed to chew.

Teach your dog that some items are appropriate for him to chew, while others are not.

Barking

A tendency to bark is to some extent inherited, and because barking was useful when hunting fox underground, your terrier's ancestors were chosen in part for their ability to sound a tallyho. Even when he's not hunting, barking is a natural means of communication for a dog, and terriers like to communicate! Your dog barks to say hello, issue a warning, invite a friend to play, and sometimes just for fun. As he interacts with people in your home, your dog quickly learns that very often he can get you to do something by barking. Think about it—he barks and you let him in, let him out, throw a ball, and feed him. You understand him most of the time, and you respond. Your dog also barks to alert you to happenings around your home—like when a stranger comes to the door, a dog passes by on the pavement, a squirrel scampers onto the front porch—and to warn or challenge intruders. Barking is a rewarding behaviour for a dog, and therefore it is sometimes hard to stop.

Most people find a reasonable amount of canine vocal activity acceptable and even comforting at times. (If you don't, please reconsider your choice of a Parson or Jack Russell Terrier.) But a dog who barks incessantly is anything but comforting. The bad news is that terriers in general do seem to think that their opinions matter. Your smart little terrier may learn that he can get you excited by barking—what fun!

Problem barking—that is, barking that exceeds reasonable levels—can usually be reduced, but you have to invest some time and effort. In the meantime, let your neighbours know that you're trying to solve the problem. Even if they haven't complained about the racket, you can be sure they've noticed it, and nothing is more annoying than a constantly barking neighbourhood dog. Also, don't leave your dog outdoors when you're not home. This is not a great idea with any dog, but it is particularly inappropriate if you own a barker.

Solution

If your dog is a big mouth, try to figure out why. Is he bored? Does he get insufficient exercise? Does he spend a lot of time alone? Is there something in your home or garden that excites him and stimulates his barking? Do you respond in ways that encourage him to continue to bark? If you find the reason for excessive barking, you're halfway to a solution.

Ways to Relieve Teething Pain

To relieve your puppy's discomfort while he's teething, give him:
- Chew toys, such as Nylabones
- Plain ice cubes or "soupsicles" made of low-sodium chicken, beef, or vegetable stock frozen into ice cubes
- A raw carrot

To help prevent excessive barking, see that your dog gets lots of daily exercise. One or two short training sessions, a good game of chase the ball, a long walk, or all of the above may help curb his barking if he's bored or full of surplus energy. Take an obedience class, even if you've taken one before. Even if your dog doesn't bark in class, and it doesn't seem that you're addressing the problem, training often has a ripple effect on a dog's behaviour. Obedience work also engages your terrier's mind, giving him more to think about than how bored he is.

Barking is also, of course, your dog's way of telling you that something's wrong. "Intruder, intruder," he tells you. On the rare occasion that the threat is a burglar, barking is good. But if it's your neighbour taking the rubbish out or working in her garden, uncontrolled barking isn't so great. Again, obedience training will help by giving you a way to direct your dog to alternative behaviours. When he starts to bark at someone, have him sit or lie down and stay. If you need to get more control, put his lead on. When he's quiet, praise and reward him. It's easy to forget this crucial part of the process—don't just tell him what he's doing wrong, but remember to tell him what he's doing right.

Although terriers have a tendency to bark, excessive barking can sometimes be reduced through training and exercise.

You can also introduce your dog to the neighbours so that they won't seem like strangers in "his" territory. Teach him that having people around is a good thing. Have the neighbour or a friend walk by your garden. If your dog stays quiet, tell him how good he is and give him a treat. Better yet, have the other person give him a treat. If he barks, tell him, "Down" and "Stay," and praise and reward him as soon as he's quiet. Repeat the process several times a day for several days, having the "intruder" come closer as your dog becomes quieter and steadier on the stay. Get as many different people as possible to help so that your dog can generalise being quiet to anyone who walks by. If your dog is indoors, you can use the same method: Have him lie down and be quiet, and praise and reward him when he complies.

Why Do Dogs Bark?

Dogs bark for a variety of reasons, including the following:
· to communicate
· to alert or warn
· for fun
· to alleviate boredom

As with all training, consistency is vital to success. Don't ignore your dog's barking one time, encourage it the next, and yell at him the time after that. Although it's unlikely you'll ever completely stop your terrier from barking—after all, he comes from a rich heritage of barkers— you should be able to teach him to be more tolerant and controllable.

Sometimes barking is part and parcel of other behavioural problems that need to be addressed before the barking will subside. Many dogs with separation anxiety bark excessively. Dogs who are highly territorial, which terriers often are, may insist on talking about it. Dogs who were not socialised well as puppies may be nervous around strangers and bark at anyone or anything as a result. A word of caution, too—don't believe the old saying that barking dogs don't bite. The only dog who has ever given me a serious bite barked like crazy, lunged, bit, and went right back to barking. (He was not a terrier!)

Some people resort to anti-bark collars that are supposed to discourage barking by administering a spray of citronella aimed at the dog's nose, or some give out a high-pitched sound. The manufacturers of anti-bark collars promise a quick end to your dog's behavioural problems.

The problem is that although anti-bark collars seem to offer a quick solution, they treat the symptoms rather than the cause. If your dog barks because he's bored, he may stop yapping but find an equally undesirable replacement. If he's anxious or afraid, an anti-bark collar will probably increase his stress level, leading to more neurotic behaviours. If he's territorial or aggressive, he may think the person or animal at which he's barking is the source of his discomfort, and he may become more aggressive.

Anti-bark collars do work on some dogs, but not all. I've heard many a dog bark while sporting a fully operational anti-bark collar. As with other behavioural problems, prevention, control, and training are always the best solutions.

Jumping Up

Do you want your dog to jump up and plant nice muddy paw prints on you trousers, rip your tights with his nails, or knock a toddler flat on the floor? Probably not. And really, your dog's goal isn't to cause problems when he jumps up. He simply likes you and wants your attention. Besides, you and other people probably reward him for the behaviour by petting him or picking him up or by getting excited and pushing him away—all acceptable results from your dog's point of view.

Solution

Clearly, you need to teach your dog that jumping up doesn't get him what he wants. To get that message across, you have to be consistent in your response when he does jump up, and you need to try to get other people who interact with your dog to cooperate in the training. If you have a puppy, start teaching him from the day you bring him home that jumping up doesn't get him picked up and cuddled. If you adopt an older terrier who has not been taught to stay off, it may take a bit longer to break his old habit, but if you stick with it, he will learn.

To prevent jumping up, be consistent with your response when the unwanted behaviour occurs.

One way to get the message across is to completely ignore your dog when he's jumping up. Fold your arms over your chest, turn your back on the dog, look up or away, and don't say a word. If you've been pushing him down before starting this method, your dog will keep trying for a while, but sooner or later he'll realise that jumping gets him a very boring human rather than an excited, active playmate, and he'll quit. When he has his four feet back on the floor, talk to him calmly and pet him. If he jumps up again, ignore him. He'll soon realise that his attempts to get your attention get the opposite result, and he'll quit.

To be successful with this approach, you have to be patient and think ahead. Don't wear anything except puppy-safe clothes around your dog until he's reliable about not jumping on you. If necessary, get up a little earlier, take care of your pup, and then confine him before you get dressed for work. When you get home, change your clothes before you let your dog out. You have to make some effort for a few weeks, but consistent training will pay off in years of living with a dog who doesn't jump on you.

Redirection, or directing your dog to perform a different behaviour, is another way of teaching him not to jump up. For this method to work, your dog must know some obedience commands (which he should learn anyway), and you must be alert and able to predict his probable behaviour. When you think he's about to jump up, direct your dog to do something else, like sit or down. When he performs as directed, praise him. Give him a treat or other reward while he's learning, and when he's reliable, simply praise him for a correct response. This method works well for many people, but there are some drawbacks. Obviously, your dog needs to understand the command you give, and if he doesn't yet understand it, you have to teach him as you go. This is fine, but yelling, "Sit, sit, SIT" at ever higher and more frantic volumes as your dog leaps up won't teach him anything except that you are excitable. That's the second problem with the method. Your smart little terrier will quickly realise that he can get people excited by jumping up—what fun!—or that he can "train" you to tell him to sit and give him a treat.

Confining a dog with separation anxiety when you're not home is important for the protection of both your dog and your possessions.

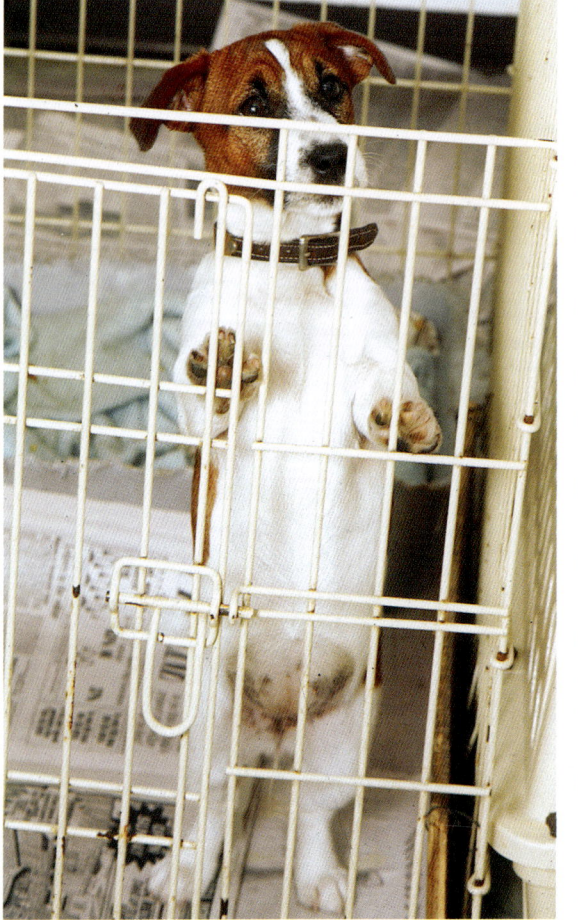

Regardless of your approach to teaching your dog not to jump up, there are a few things you should not do. Don't put your hands on your dog to push him away or down, and don't follow the pushing down with petting. Attention is what he wants, and being pushed or petted rewards him for jumping. Wait until he gets off on his own, and then pet him. Don't knee, kick, or hit your dog for jumping up, either. Unless you're very coordinated, you probably won't connect, but if you do you could seriously injure your dog. You will also teach him not to trust you, and you could provoke a defensive response. You'll get farther faster if you take the time to teach your dog that being polite gets him what he wants, and jumping up does not.

Fear and Anxiety

Separation anxiety is a condition in which a dog becomes frightened, worried, and agitated in his owner's absence. Although different dogs behave in different ways, common symptoms of separation anxiety include barking, whining, or howling, pacing the floor, salivating or vomiting, urinating or defecating inappropriately, or destructiveness.

Solution

Many people unwittingly create or contribute to separation anxiety by their own behaviour when leaving and arriving home. If you act like being away from your dog is a terrible, traumatic thing, he'll will pick up on your attitude and believe your absence is reason for serious worry. To avoid teaching him this, don't make a fuss over your dog when you leave or come back. Put him in his crate 10 to 15 minutes before you plan to leave so that he can relax. Give him a special treat that he gets only when you go out without him, such as a special chew toy or hollow bone stuffed with soft cheese or peanut butter and dry food, for example. Once your dog is in his crate, go about your business and ignore him. If you have a puppy, you'll need to get him out to relieve himself as soon as you come home, but if your dog is older and shows signs of separation anxiety, don't let him out immediately when you get home. Wait until he calms down, and then let him out but don't make a big fuss. You can coo and cuddle later.

Don't make too big a deal of leaving or coming home, or you may make your dog anxious.

Confining a dog with separation anxiety when you're not home is important for the protection of both your dog and your possessions. An anxious dog can cause a lot of damage and can injure himself or ingest things he shouldn't. Most dogs feel secure in their crates, and they're certainly safer. If your dog isn't already crate trained, get a crate and teach him to be comfortable in it. Always crate him when you leave. If you give him a safe chew toy, he'll have a way to relieve his stress without hurting himself or anything else.

Obedience training also helps build confidence in an anxious dog. Teach your dog the stay command, and have him practice staying for different lengths of time while you go about your regular activities at home. Work up to stays of half an hour or longer, and teach him to stay even when you leave the room. (Don't forget to go back and release him!) Staying in one place

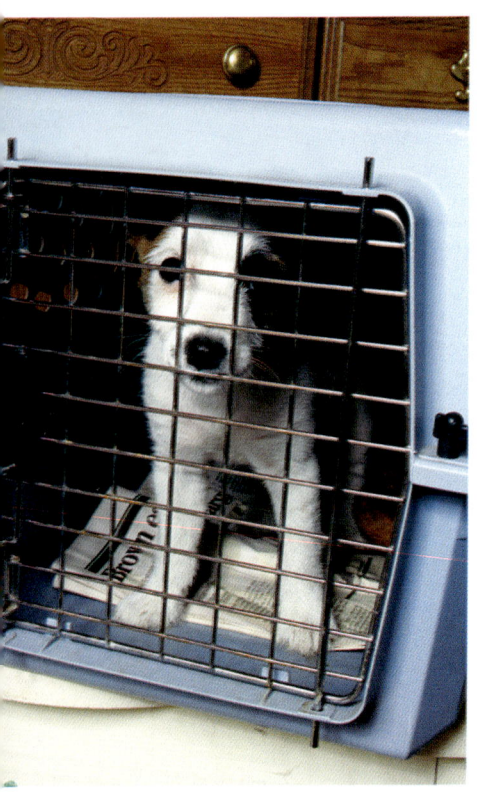

Be sure that your dog has a view of the room when you leave him in his crate, and that he has some toys to occupy him.

while you move around will teach your dog that he doesn't have to be right next to you to be safe. Crate your dog sometimes when you're home, too, so that he'll know it's a safe haven whether you're at home or away.

If possible, work out how long it is after you leave that your dog becomes overly anxious. Then, try leaving for periods shorter than that and calmly returning. If he starts to howl when you've been gone five minutes, stay away for three minutes and come back, but stay calm and don't fuss over him. If he stayed calm, let him out of his crate and quietly praise and reward him with a little treat or play session. If he was agitated, ignore him until he calms down. Don't reward him for being upset. Try these short reconditioning sessions on weekends and in the evening. Even if you can't stay home for a month to help your dog conquer his fears, you can reduce his anxiety by teaching him that you won't always be gone for hours, and no matter how long you're gone, you will always come back and nothing bad will happen to him in the meantime.

Where your dog spends his alone time may make a difference, too. If he enjoys looking out the window, try placing his crate where he can see out. If that makes him more agitated, move him away from the windows. Voices or music soothe some dogs, so try leaving a radio or television on with the volume down low. Your pup might also like to cling to something that smells like you— maybe an old sweatshirt that you haven't laundered since you last wore it. One of my dogs used to sleep with one of my shoes. If your dog is a chewer or ripper upper, don't give him anything that can hurt him or vice versa, but if he's not, a "little bit of you" might comfort him in your absence. If you have to be away for very long hours, consider paying someone to come in during the day to let your dog out for a while, especially if he seems to become anxious after you've been gone several hours.

If separation anxiety continues to be a problem after you've tried to recondition his behaviour, talk to your vet or a qualified animal behaviourist. They may identify specific factors affecting your dog and your situation and be able to create an effective treatment plan that addresses those factors. Anti-anxiety medication can be prescribed in extreme cases, but drugs aren't usually a good long-term solution. Some people also report success with herbs, flower essences, acupuncture, and various physical therapies. There's no scientific evidence proving their effectiveness, but most won't hurt your dog, so they might be worth a try.

Mouthing and Biting

Terriers can be quick to use their teeth in their own defence, so it's extremely important to lay down some rules of interaction from the very beginning. Rule number one, which your puppy should begin to learn from your very first encounter, is that canine teeth do not belong on human skin, even in play. There's a good chance you'll need to teach this rule not only to your dog but also to your human family, particularly younger children, who love rough play.

It's not hard to figure out why puppies like to mouth and nibble us—when they play with their toys and with one another, they bite, tug, grab, lick, and pull. Use of his mouth comes naturally to your puppy, and he'll probably mouth you until you teach him not to. A mentally sound puppy doesn't mean to hurt you, but puppy teeth are sharp, and you aren't protected by fur like his mother and siblings. For his future well-being, and that of everyone he meets, your pup must learn that he simply may not use his teeth on human beings.

Consistency

Consistency is essential to success when teaching your dog not to jump up. If you ignore your bouncing dog part of the time but reward him at other times by talking, pushing him off, and getting excited, your dog will have a merry time and continue to jump up to get you to "play."

Solution

I've found two methods to be very effective when dealing with mouthing and biting. First, shunning is a very effective way of telling a social animal that he's done something wrong, and as with jumping up, if you teach your pup that mouthing and biting are counterproductive, he'll stop. To teach him this, you need to get up, walk away, and ignore your dog for a minute or so the instant he puts his teeth on you. Then go back to what you were doing with him—playing, gently rubbing his tummy, or anything else that doesn't encourage him to mouth you. Every time he does, get up and ignore him again. If he pulls on your clothes or bites your ankles, leave the room for a minute and ignore him. Then come back and try again. Most puppies will quickly make the connection and keep their teeth to themselves.

Another effective way to redirect mouthy behaviour is to give your pup something to put in his mouth other than you. If he mouths you when you're petting him or playing, gently offer him a toy and continue to pet him. He'll soon figure out that hands are good for belly rubs and ear scratches but not for chewing. If he insists on mouthing and biting you instead of the toy, use the shunning method I already outlined.

Some puppies learn very quickly, while others take a little longer. If ignoring your pup for short periods doesn't have the desired effect, leave him completely alone for a minute or so. Take the toys with you if necessary so that he has no fun without you. Then return and resume play. For this method to work, everyone in your household must use it consistently.

Sharp puppy teeth are annoying and painful and can easily break skin, but mouthing is nevertheless normal puppy behaviour that pups simply need to stop. A lot of puppy play sounds pretty nasty—puppies growl and snarl and bark at each other—but it is play. Think of it as a canine version of kids on a playground, with growls replacing yelling. The puppy isn't trying to hurt anyone—he just wants to have fun.

True aggression, including serious growling, guarding, and biting, is something else entirely. It is not normal and is potentially dangerous to people and other pets. If your dog growls or bares his teeth at you or any other member of your family, snaps, or guards his food, toys, bed, or anything else from you, talk to his breeder, your vet, or your obedience instructor. You might be misinterpreting normal puppy antics, and it's important to know that before you label your pup as "aggressive." But an occasional puppy or dog truly is unacceptably aggressive, and such a pup will not improve on his own. If your dog is aggressive, or if you're not sure his behaviour is normal, get help from a dog trainer or behaviourist who is qualified to deal with aggression, or return the pup to the breeder. In the meantime, don't take any chances, especially if you have children.

It's important to remember that young dogs are similar in many ways to young humans. Puppies and adolescents sometimes get grumpy when they're tired, just like young children. If your puppy is getting really silly or a bit grumpy, he may just be tired. And like a child, he doesn't have the sense to put himself to bed, so it's up to you to put him in his crate and let him rest. He may complain for a minute or two, but then he'll go to sleep.

Whatever you do, *do not* respond to mouthing or nipping (or anything else, for that matter) by slapping or grabbing your dog's face. Violence doesn't teach your dog what you want him to learn and nearly always causes more problems. Most terriers don't like being threatened, and your terrier may try to defend himself with a real bite. Even if your dog isn't that tough, he may bite out of fear or run away or avoid you. Either way, you now have a bigger problem to deal with.

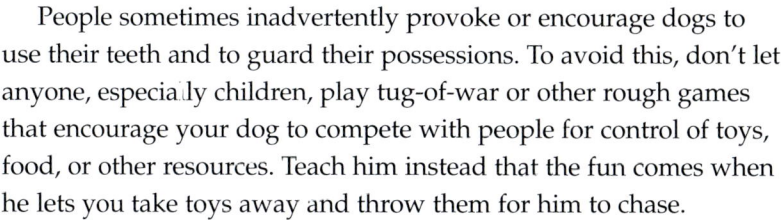

Puppies should be redirected to interact with toys rather than get too mouthy with people.

People sometimes inadvertently provoke or encourage dogs to use their teeth and to guard their possessions. To avoid this, don't let anyone, especially children, play tug-of-war or other rough games that encourage your dog to compete with people for control of toys, food, or other resources. Teach him instead that the fun comes when he lets you take toys away and throw them for him to chase.

Even if you think your dog is utterly reliable, a responsible adult should supervise all interaction between him and children. Supervision means that the adult is in a position to intervene immediately if necessary. Training, especially "no teeth training," should be done by an adult. Children often react to rough puppy play by screaming, jumping around, pushing the puppy away, and getting excited, which will excite your puppy even more. He'll think the kids are having as much fun as he is, and he'll keep jumping and nipping. Play involving kids and pups can get out of control very quickly, and kids and pups can both end up injured or frightened, so train them all to play nicely and supervise them closely.

Resource Guarding

Resource guarding refers to behaviour aimed at keeping control of a resource, which is anything that has value for the dog, including food, a toy, a dog bed, the couch, and even a person. It's a common problem in dogs who are not taught that it's unacceptable behaviour and that people control the good stuff. Left unchecked, resource guarding can become dangerous. (If your dog has already developed a pattern of aggressive resource guarding, especially if he has snapped or bitten, get help immediately from a qualified trainer or behaviourist.) Fortunately, most dogs can be taught not to guard things from people, especially if you start training when they're puppies.

Solution

Rough play that encourages your dog to challenge you or keep things from you teaches him that it's okay to do so. A safer, more sensible approach to life with a terrier is to teach him from the day he comes home that you control all the good things in his life—

Don't play games like tug-of-war with a dog who is prone to resource guarding.

food, toys, access to play, and exercise. You don't have to bully your dog, but you do need to be consistent and give him basic obedience training. Dogs are not democratic beings; they respect authority and are much happier when a strong but benevolent leader is in control.

As your puppy matures, you can expect him to try to climb the social ladder within his pack (your human and animal household). When that happens, you need to reassert your authority. If he challenges you for a toy, his food, or your favourite chair, he should immediately lose his privileges. The toy disappears for a while (all toys if necessary). Your dog should get his dinner a few morsels at a time, and he should have to earn each portion by responding to a command such as sit or down. He should also stay off the furniture, including your bed, until he accepts that he's there by your approval, not by his divine right. It's also a good idea to take the adolescent pup through another obedience class to continue his training and socialisation.

Aggression

True aggression in dogs is characterised by serious growling, aggressive posturing, and biting directed at people or other animals, and it can have any of several causes. Some dogs simply have bad temperaments, while other dogs suffer from medical problems or pain, which can contribute to aggressive behaviour. A dog's life history and experience can also lead to aggression.

Whatever the cause, an aggressive dog—one who threatens to bite, tries to bite, or does bite—is dangerous. Don't underestimate the damage a dog, even a small one, can inflict if he means to. If your dog behaves aggressively, get qualified professional help immediately, and take measures to protect those around him in the meantime.

Solution

The first step in managing aggression is to rule out a physical problem. Schedule a thorough physical examination, including a full thyroid panel (not just a thyroid screening), as hypothyroidism (low thyroid function) and other medical conditions can contribute to aggressive behaviour. Be sure you tell your vet about your dog's behaviour, and ask whether other tests would be useful. Neutering reduces aggression in both males and females, especially if it's done before the dog reaches sexual maturity, so if your terrier is sexually intact, schedule him or her to be castrated or spayed. When a physical cause for aggression can be identified, it may be possible to stop the behaviour with treatment.

Having a well-behaved dog requires an investment of time, effort, and money, but you'll both be happier if you train your dog. Like all intelligent beings, your terrier will thrive on learning new things, and he will respect and love you more for teaching him what you want and expect from him. Training is one of the most loving things you can do for your dog in return for the love he gives you.

Doggy Discipline
When children misbehave, they lose privileges. The same principle applies to dogs who misbehave. When trouble starts, immediately stop what you're doing with your dog. Take away any toys you may be playing with, and put him in his crate for some quiet time. When he has settled down, do some training with him to reinforce that he should be listening and responding to you.

Warning Signs

We sometimes hear that a dog bit someone "with no warning." In reality, that rarely happens. Dogs almost always give warnings, sometimes increasing the warning level over the course of several incidents. Unfortunately, people—especially children—don't always understand canine warning signals. If your dog's hair stands on end (especially along his spine), if he stands very erect with his legs stiff and his tail straight up, or if he growls and bares his teeth, he is flashing a doggy red light. He is not bluffing, and his behaviour is not cute or funny. If your dog displays any of these warning signals, especially against people, get help immediately from your dog's breeder, your vet, or a qualified canine behaviourist.

7

ADVANCED TRAINING AND ACTIVITIES
for Your Parson or Jack Russell Terrier

The Parson and Jack Russell Terriers' versatility makes them very popular participants in many canine sports. Their small size makes them quite portable, and their big attitude makes them serious contenders in most activities. If you enjoy the time you spend training your dog and being with other "dog people," you might want to try out some of the activities introduced in this chapter.

NONCOMPETITIVE ACTIVITIES

If you're like most dog owners, you brought home a dog to be your companion only. Being a loyal friend is certainly what dogs do best, and even top competitors should be companions above all. But it's fun, too, to channel the energy, intelligence, and attitude that is part and parcel of the terrier into activities that get the two of you out of the house and garden and into the wide world of doggy activities. Let's look at some of the possibilities.

Walking, Jogging, and Running

If you use good sense and take a few precautions, walking, jogging, and running are safe and pleasurable activities for dog and human alike. They're also inexpensive—just put on your shoes and your dog's collar and lead, and off you go. But before you do, let's see how you can keep your outings as safe and enjoyable as possible.

First, be sure you and your dog have no health problems that preclude this kind of exercise. If you haven't had check-ups in a while, do so. If your dog is overweight, put him on a diet and start out slowly with walks. If your dog is out of condition, or if he's elderly or has been ill or injured, ask your vet about appropriate speed and distance. Check your dog's feet, too. His nails should be trimmed so that they don't hit the ground when he walks, and his pads should be in good condition.

Your terrier needs good lead skills before you take him walking or jogging away from your own property or training class, and in any case, whoever walks the dog must be able to control the dog. Children are often keen to walk the dog, but if the child can't control him under all circumstances, don't let her walk the dog without a responsible adult. Safe walking isn't just a matter of controlling your own dog, and some walking hazards (encounters with stray dogs, for instance) can be difficult even for adults to manage. Such situations can be even more dangerous for a child. The terrier's strong instinct to chase, and his scrappiness with strange dogs, can create serious problems that a child may not be able to manage safely.

A lot of people are tempted to let their dogs off lead in public, but there are many good reasons not to do so. For one thing, it's illegal in many places. Consideration for other people and animals and for your dog's safety is another important reason to keep your dog on lead. Be sure his collar fits properly so that he can't slip out of it, or if he has learned to do so, use a martingale-style collar that tightens when he pulls against the lead. Be sure the bolt on your lead is secure and that the lead is in good condition as well. Keep a firm grip on your lead, but don't slip your hand through the loop; a quick jerk by a lunging dog can break your wrist. Teach children not to slide their hands through the loop or put a lead around their necks or waists.

If children want to take dogs for walks, an adult should supervise.

Try to limit your outings to early in the morning or in the evening when the temperature is lower. Concrete and tarmac get very hot in the sun and can burn your dog's footpads. They can also reflect enough heat to cause heatstroke. (See Chapter 8 for more information.) Dogs can sunburn, too, and the white areas of your terrier, particularly on his nose, are especially vulnerable. Be sure to avoid areas where pesticides or herbicides have been used. If your dog does walk though a treated area, wash his feet with warm water and dog shampoo when you get home to keep him from absorbing or ingesting toxic chemicals. If you like to walk or jog in the dark, make yourselves visible to drivers—wear light colours or reflective clothing, and put a reflective collar or vest on your dog.

Be a Good Neighbour

Please be a good neighbour and pick up after your dog when walking, jogging, or running with him. You can purchase disposable pooper-scoopers, but plastic bags or disposable plastic gloves are cheaper and work just as well. To use one:
1. Turn the bag inside out over your hand, or put the glove on.
2. Pick up the poop with your "plastic hand."
3. Pull the edge of the bag or glove down over your hand, capturing the poop, and pull your hand out.
4. Seal the bag or tie a knot in the glove.
5. Dispose of the bag or glove in a proper receptacle (carry it home if necessary).

Very cold weather holds dangers, too. Russells are hardy dogs, but in extremely low temperatures, they can suffer from hypothermia or frostbite if they stay out too long. Chemicals and salt used to melt ice can irritate your dog's feet and can be toxic if he licks them off, so if salt or other chemicals have been used where your dog will be stepping, wash his feet with warm water after every walk.

Hiking and Backpacking

Terriers are terrific hiking and backpacking partners; they have the stamina for long walks and can show you things you might otherwise miss. Your terrier is alert enough to keep anyone and anything from sneaking up on you. He's small enough that you can carry him if necessary but sturdy enough to learn to wear a small backpack and carry a small supply of his food and water. (Build him up slowly to carrying weight.) He can even carry his own plastic baggies and bring back his bagged faeces to keep the countryside clean.

Plan ahead for your outdoor adventures and you'll have more fun. First, check that dogs are allowed where you want to hike, because they're not allowed in some parks and nature reserves. If your dog is permitted, keep him under control at all times. Leads are required in most places, and even if they're not, a lead will keep your terrier safe and prevent him from disturbing wildlife or your fellow hikers.

Of course, your dog should be in good health and his vaccinations up to date before you take him hiking. Ask your vet about recommended vaccines. Natural areas harbour bacterial and viral diseases that your dog won't be exposed to around your neighbourhood. Protect him from ticks with an effective tick repellant

Your dog may enjoy a variety of outdoor adventures, such as earthdog.

and killer. After an excursion, check your dog thoroughly for ticks, which can 'hide' in your dog's coat.

Your dog's nails should be trimmed nice and short before embarking on a hike, with any rough edges that could catch and tear smoothed with a nail grinder or file. Check his feet and pads for cuts or scrapes before, every so often during, and after a hike. If your dog is overweight or out of shape, start with shorter walks before setting out on a longer journey.

The right equipment will make your outings safer and more pleasant. As always, your dog needs a collar that fits well and is in good condition. You should also check that his identification tag is securely attached. A nylon lead is a good choice for hiking in wet conditions. If you use leather, which is easier on the hands than nylon, be sure to waterproof it, and if it gets wet or dirty, clean it when you get home. Retractable leads are good in some situations, but they tend to wrap around trees and undergrowth, and some parks require dogs to be on leads 6 feet (1.8 m) or shorter. It's a good idea to carry a spare collar and lead "just in case."

Don't forget to take clean drinking water, and bring a bowl for your dog or teach him to drink from a squirt bottle. Offer your dog water at regular intervals to prevent dehydration and overheating. Don't let him drink from streams and other water sources along the way if you can help it—they're often contaminated with bacteria and chemicals. Lightweight collapsible bowls are available in pet supply stores for easy packing.

In warm weather, hike in the early morning or evening and avoid the hottest parts of the day if possible. Dogs can overheat quickly, and heatstroke is potentially fatal. If you will be at higher altitudes than your normal environment, allow time for your bodies to adjust, and schedule extra time for breaks. Proper hydration helps fend off altitude sickness, so be sure that both you and your dog drink lots of water. Pack a few lightweight first-aid supplies, too—tweezers can be useful if your dog picks up a thorn or tick, and antiseptic cleansing towels and a topical antibiotic can also come in handy. Don't forget a good insect repellant!

Dogs have been banned from many recreational areas, so we all need to do our part to keep them welcome in the places still open to them. Don't hike with a dog you can't control or one who is a threat to people or other dogs. Even a small dog can be frightening to some people, so teach your dog to sit or lie quietly beside the trail when other hikers want to pass.

If you're hiking alone with your dog, be sure to tell a reliable friend where you're going and how long you'll be gone, and let her know when you get back.

THE KC GOOD CITIZEN DOG SCHEME

The Kennel Club's Good Citizen Dog Scheme is designed to promote and reward well-behaved dogs as community members. There are four levels to aim for: puppy foundation, bronze, silver, and gold. The tests focus on basic good manners and include the following:

During the Canine Good Citizen test, your dog will demonstrate various obedience skills on command.

1. **Accepting a friendly stranger:** The friendly stranger will approach and greet the dog's handler. The dog must remain quiet.

2. **Sitting politely for petting:** This will occur while a friendly stranger pets the dog's head and body.

3. **Appearance and grooming:** This involves two steps. First, the evaluator checks that the dog is clean, groomed, and in good condition. Then, the dog must permit a stranger to comb or brush him and check his ears and front feet.

4. **Out for a walk:** This requires the dog to walk quietly on a loose lead, making several turns and stops.

5. **Walking through a crowd:** This step requires the dog and handler to walk politely around and among at least three people.

6. **Sit and down on command and staying in place:** The dog is required to sit, lie down, and stay on command.

7. **Coming when called**: This step requires the dog to stay on command and then come

If you have a special dog who is especially well mannered with people, consider getting involved in animal-assisted therapy with him.

when called from a set distance.

8. **Reaction to another dog:** The dog should react with only casual interest when meeting another dog and handler.

9. **Reaction to distraction:** The dog should react calmly to two common distractions (for instance, a chair falling over, a jogger running by, a wheeled cart passing by, or a dropped crutch or cane).

10. **Supervised separation:** The dog should remain calm when left with the evaluator while his handler goes out of sight for three minutes.

During the tests, the dog must wear a properly fitted collar made of leather, fabric, or chain, and he will be on lead for most of the exercises the dog must also have an up-to-date ID tag with your name, and contact details. Remember to bring your dog's brush or comb for the grooming portion.

Don't give up if your dog doesn't pass the test on the first attempt— you'll know what you need to work on in the future! Keep training, have fun, and try again later.

ANIMAL-ASSISTED ACTIVITIES AND THERAPY

The term "therapy dog" is used to indicate a dog who works with people in a positive, beneficial environment. In most cases, you and your dog will visit people in a variety of situations, such as nursing homes, literacy and reading programmes, hospitals, and schools. No professional therapist participates in the visits, and no formal measurements are made of the dog's effect on people's progress or treatment.

The aim of animal-assisted therapy visits is to allow people to interact with a dog in an organised, but informal, situation. Sometimes, residents or patients will want to talk to you. Others will be content simply to pet the dog. If you and your terrier like people and enjoy volunteering, you both might find therapy work extremely rewarding.

Many facilities will welcome your dog when you can state that you have accreditation. In the UK, the governing body for therapy dogs is Pets as Therapy (PAT). For detailed information on registering your Shih Tzu as a PAT dog, visit their website, which you can find at www.petsastherapy.org.

A dog must be a minimum of nine months of age before applying to be a therapy dog. Pets as Therapy will send you the application forms. The organisation has trained evaluators working throughout the country. If your dog appears to be suitable, an evaluator will make arrangements to visit your dog and assess him.

It is important to ensure that a therapy dog is absolutely reliable, so a number of assessments are made. In most cases the test is conducted on neutral territory so the evaluator can see if the dog has the confidence to work and co-operate in unfamiliar surroundings. The evaluator will ask the dog and handler to perform the following tests:

- Walk on a loose lead
- Remain under control despite distractions
- Remain calm and not react to loud, sudden noises
- Accept all-over grooming
- Accept all-over touching and handling, even when it is a little clumsy
- Leave a toy or treat on command
- Take a treat gently

Assistance Dogs

Therapy dogs should not be confused with assistance dogs, who are trained intensively to work as guide dogs for the blind, hearing dogs for the deaf, seizure-alert dogs, dogs for the disabled, and so on. Assistance dogs have legal rights; therapy dogs do not.

Therapy work can be extremely rewarding, but it can also be stressful. Your dog will probably make it clear if he isn't enjoying the visits, but you need to be alert to subtle signs that he's unhappy. Some dogs like certain kinds of visits but not others, and dogs can suffer burnout just like humans can. Sometimes a different type of work does the trick, but sometimes your dog just needs a short break.

If your dog is really not enjoying his visits, you may need to consider retiring him. It's a wonderful feeling to see your dog bring joy to people in difficult circumstances, but your own dog's well-being should always come first. Keep in mind, too, that not all terriers are suited to therapy work, which requires a dog to be calm and receptive to all kinds of people, and sometimes rough petting or other unexpected or odd occurrences.

Racing is one organised sport that offers you and your dog the opportunity to achieve a goal together.

CANINE SPORTS FOR FUN AND GLORY

Whatever your reasons for continuing to train your dog beyond basic obedience, you'll find that the more you work with your dog, the stronger the bond between the two of you. Advanced training will also direct your terrier's physical and mental energy into acceptable pursuits and will let you spend time with people who understand how you feel about your dog. Let's look at some of the activities open to Parson and Jack Russell Terriers.

Obedience

The objective of dog obedience is to demonstrate teamwork between handler and dog. Terriers can and do succeed in competitive obedience, but you need to remember that they are bred to work independently when hunting and that obedience training a terrier can therefore be challenging. Like many intelligent dogs, Russells are easily bored and will not perform the same exercise over and over again, so you will need to find ways to make the work fun and interesting for your dog.

In the UK, competitive obedience is dominated by Border Collies and working sheepdogs, with some German Shepherd Dogs, Golden Retrievers and Labrador Retrievers. However, there is no reason why you should not have a go with your Russell—as long as you can retain a sense of humour.

There are various levels of obedience in the UK, with each covering a range of abilities. These are pre-beginners, beginners, novice, class A, class B and class C. Each level becomes progressively more demanding. There will be a winner in each level of class.

The pre-beginners class is for the least experienced in the obedience world. Competitors must perform five different obedience exercises, totalling 75 points. Points are deducted for faults within each exercise. The exercises include walking to heel, both on and off lead, recall, sit-stay, and down-stay.

The beginners class is for those who have succeeded at pre-beginners. This class includes all the exercises from the pre-beginners class but also includes retrieving an article. This takes the potential points total to 100 points.

The novice class contains all the elements from the beginners class, and also includes a temperament test, in which the judge will run his hands over the dog. The points total for this class is also 100 points.

Class A is similar to the novice class, although the sit-stay and the down-stay exercises are longer and less encouragement and help is allowed from the handler. There is also a scent discrimination test, in which 6 cloths are laid down. The dog has to select the single cloth that has been marked with the handler's scent. There is a total of 150 points on offer in this class.

Class B is more involved than class A. The off-lead heelwork performed in this class must include changes of pace. There is an additional exercise known as the sendaway, drop and recall. In this exercise the handler must send the dog away in one direction, order him to drop to the floor, then call him back. As in class A, there are also exercises for the retrieve, scent discrimination, sit-stay and down-stay. There is also a stand-stay. The inclusion of additional exercises takes the points total to 200.

Class C is the master class of obedience competition, and offers a total of 300 points. It contains many of the elements of class B but with many of the exercises being longer in duration and with the judges allowing less room for error. One of the hardest exercises in class C is distance control, in which the handler must get the dog to perform six different exercises while dog and handler are at least 10 paces apart.

JRTs and KC Events

If your Russell is not registered with the Kennel Club, you can still participate in KC events if you apply to enrol him on the Working Dogs Activity register.

There are three different types of obedience tests or shows. These are limited obedience shows, open obedience shows, and championship obedience shows. Competition becomes successively more difficult through these tests. There may be many different classes scheduled at each show, from pre-beginners through to class C.

Championship classes are open to anyone and they offer a special award—the Kennel Club's obedience challenge certificate. These certificates are available only to dogs winning in class C events. Once a dog has achieved three obedience challenge certificates or 'tickets' under three different judges, he is awarded the title Obedience Champion.

Rally Obedience

Rally obedience is the new kid on the block of competitive canine sports. At present, it is not available in the UK, but the chances are that it will find its way here before long. Rally obedience is a hybrid of competitive obedience and agility, which requires the handler and dog to execute a course consisting of stations at which they must demonstrate specific skills. In January 2005, the AKC began to offer competition and titles in rally obedience.

At the Novice level in AKC rally, all exercises are performed on lead, and to earn the Rally Novice (RN) title, the dog must earn qualifying scores at three trials. He may then move up to the Rally Advanced class, in which all exercises are performed off lead, including one jump (broad jump, high jump, or bar jump). When the dog has earned three qualifying scores in Rally Advanced classes, he may move on to Rally Excellent, in which all exercises except the Honor Exercise are performed off lead. A Rally Excellent course includes two jumps and an on-lead Honor Exercise, in which he must sit or down at the judge's direction while another dog performs the entire course. To earn the Rally Excellent (RE) title, the dog must earn three qualifying scores.

After a dog earns the RE title, he may continue to work toward the Rally Advanced Excellent (RAE) title by qualifying in both the Rally Advanced B Class and the Rally Excellent B Class at ten trials.

Agility

Agility made its debut as a canine sport at Crufts in 1978, and since then it has become the fastest growing dog sport in the world.

Size, speed and physical agility make the Russell a natural at this sport, which is basically a timed run over an obstacle course.

The dogs go through a course that is either a *standard course*, which has a number of contact obstacles (such as A-frames, seesaws, or dog walks), plus items such as weave poles, a pause table (where dogs have to Stay to show control), tyre jumps, and tunnels. The *Jumpers* class doesn't have contact obstacles or a pause table, which slow the dog down. This is a very fast course.

His size, speed, and physical aptitude make the Parson and Jack Russell Terriers a natural at agility.

Dogs progress from starters level, to novice, intermediate and advanced level. At each level, the courses are tougher, with more obstacles to navigate and more complicated courses to run.

In the UK, dogs are not eligble for competition until they are 18 months of age. This ruling is for the safety and well-being of the dog, as before this age many breeds are still growing and their joints could easily be damaged.

The challenge of Agility is to be able to control your dog in a wide open area, and direct him to go where you want. It looks easy enough, but courses are set with twists, turns and sometimes with deliberate traps, which can tempt your dog to take the wrong course. If a dog takes the wrong course he is eliminated. He loses points for refusals, knocked poles, and missed contact points. The winner is the dog who completes a clear round in the fastest time. Even if you never consider competing, you and your dog should consider taking an agility class. It's a great opportunity for you and your Russell to go out and have a terrific time together.

Finding Out About Agility

If you want to find out more about Agility, go to the Kennel Club website (www.the-kennel-club.org.uk) or have a look at a specialist site such as www.agilityclub.co.uk or www.agilityeye.co.uk.

Don't Forget

It's easy to get so wound up in the competitive side of a sport that we forget how we got involved in the first place. The real prize to be won in dog sports is the time you and your dog spend enjoying one another's company and learning about one another, win or lose.

Tracking, Trailing and Locating

One skill you don't need to teach your terrier is how to follow his nose. In tracking, your job is to teach your dog which scent track to follow and then to learn to trust him while he works. Tracking requires a considerable amount of time, and you have to be in reasonably good shape to follow your dog over all sorts of terrain. But if you enjoy being outdoors, tracking is terrific fun. It's fascinating to watch a dog do work that comes naturally to him and will forever be a mystery to us humans.

In the UK, tracking with small breed dogs is a neglected sport. The reason is that it is not a sport in its own right, but is included in Working Trials. This sport involved agility and manwork sections, which small breeds cannot take part in.

In the US, AKC tracking tests are designed to test your dog's ability to recognise and follow human scent. Before you can enter a tracking test, you must first get written certification from an AKC tracking judge stating that within the 12 months prior to the date of the tracking test, your dog passed a certification test simulating the conditions of an actual TD test. To earn the title Tracking Dog (TD), your dog must pass a tracking test. He can then proceed to the Tracking Dog Excellent tracking test to earn the title Tracking Dog Excellent (TDX), or a Variable Surface tracking test to earn the Variable Surface Tracking (VST) title. A Champion Tracker (CT) is a dog who has earned all three AKC tracking titles. ASCA also offers a tracking programme through which your dog can earn the ASCA TD and TDX.

Earth Events

The word "terrier" comes from the Latin *terra*, or ground. A terrier hunts quarry underground. Like tracking, earthdog and earth work events use the dog's instinctive abilities to perform a very natural task—in this case, the dog's ability and desire to follow and "work" quarry through close, dark spaces.

At the present time, the Kennel Club does not run earth dog tests for terriers. In the US, the AKC earthdog programme tests the dog's instincts and ability through courses designed to simulate hunting conditions. Some courses consist of actual underground tunnels, while others use aboveground passages through construction materials such as straw bales. The AKC offers earthdog titles at four levels: Introduction to Quarry (for beginning handlers and dogs), Junior Earthdog (JE), Senior Earthdog (SE), and Master Earthdog (ME). The quarry, normally adult rats, are caged and often go right on munching their veggies despite the racket when the dog finds them. Sometimes artificial quarry are used instead.

The JRTCA Go-To-Ground (GTG) programme was designed test the dog's ability to work underground in simulated hunting conditions. The specific requirements vary at different levels of competition, but at all levels the dog runs through an artificial "den" consisting of a tunnel built most often of wood that ends at a grate behind which is the quarry, normally a caged rat. To qualify, the dog must "mark" the quarry by barking, whining, scratching, or otherwise clearly indicating that he's found it within a certain amount of time from when he's released into the tunnel. Classes are available for puppies and adults at novice, open, and certificate levels.

Working Certificates

The JRTCA gives out three types of certificates for working terriers. The Natural Hunting Certificate Below Ground in the Field is the most prestigious of the working certificates and is awarded to

Earthdog uses a terrier's instinctive abilities to follow quarry through close, dark spaces.

JRTCA-registered or -recorded terriers who, on their own, locate and mark quarry in a natural den and either bolt or draw (chase or pull) the quarry from the den or stay with the quarry until it is dug out. A dog may earn the certificate more than once on different acceptable quarry, which include red fox, grey fox, woodchuck, raccoon, badger, and in some circumstances, opossum. A terrier who earns three or more Natural Hunting Certificates Below Ground on different quarry earns the JRTCA Bronze Working Terrier Medallion for Special Merit in the Field. The JRTCA also awards the Sporting Certificate to Jack Russells who successfully work less-threatening or above-ground quarry, and the Trial Certificate to Jack Russells who earn scores of 100 percent in the Open Class at a JRTCA-sanctioned Go-to-Ground trial.

Racing

Racing events are nothing if not exciting for both the dogs and the spectators. In the UK, this is not a recognised Kennel Club sport, but there are some informal events organised. In the US, the JRTCA offers racing events in which terriers chase a lure, usually a piece of scented fur pulled by a lure-pulling machine down a straight track of at least 150 feet (45.7 m). They finish by running through a hole in a stack of straw or hay bales. Both flat races and hurdle (steeplechase) races are offered. The dogs wear muzzles to protect the other dogs and the people who catch them at the end of the race from being bitten in the excitement. Classes are arranged by sex and age, and races are often run in heats, semi-finals, and finals; a championship race in each division pits the winners of the flat and hurdle races against one another.

The energetic, athletic Parson and Jack Russell Terriers will love playing flying disc.

Flyball

If you want to witness uninhibited canine excitement, visit a flyball tournament. Dogs love flyball, a sport in which they run relay races as four-dog teams. Russells are particularly popular with flyball fans because of their size, speed, and enthusiasm.

In the United Kingdom dogs compete as members of teams of four. Each team member races over four hurdles, hits a pedal on a box to release a tennis ball, snatches the ball from the air, and races back over the hurdles to the starting line. The first team to run all four dogs without errors wins the heat. Individual dogs earn points toward flyball titles based on the team's time.

Flying Disc

Many people like to throw flying discs for their dogs to chase and catch, but for some people, disc sports are more than a back garden pastime. The size, enthusiasm, and athleticism of the Parson and Jack Russell Terriers make them naturals in this sport.

In the UK, there are some demonstrations of disc catching, but it is not recognised as a sport in its own right. Canine disc events throughout the world are sanctioned by the International Disc Dog Handlers' Association (IDDHA). Before you can compete for titles, you and your dog must

demonstrate basic teamwork by successfully completing a test programme. You may then compete for titles, including the BDD (Basic Disc Dog), ADD (Advanced Disc Dog), MDD (Master Disc Dog), CSF (Combined Skills Freestyle title), and DDX (Disc Dog Expert).

If you enjoy throwing flying discs for your dog to chase, you might want to consider participating on a more competitive level.

Dancing With Dogs

Have you ever wanted to dance with your dog? Now you can dance the night away and compete for titles and prizes to boot. The relatively new sport of canine musical freestyle combines obedience and dance to demonstrate teamwork and rapport between dog and handler. The handlers and many of the dogs wear costumes as they perform carefully choreographed routines set to music. Both handler and dog are judged on several parameters. These include:

- Content of routine
- Accuracy
- Overall impression

There are different types of routine that are judged in different classes. Heelwork to Music, as the name suggests, must contain a percentage of close work, with the dog working in a variety of positions, such as left of the handler, right, in front, behind, and to the side. Freestyle routines are more flamboyant, as the dog can work at any distance from the handler, and they often include spectacular moves.

In the UK, the sport is recognised by the Kennel Club and

competitions are held throughout the year. Competitors begin in starters and work their way up through nove and intermediate to advanced level. There is a competition held annually at Crufts that draws big crowds. If you want to find out more about dancing with dog, go to the Kennel Club website—www.the-kennel-club.org.uk or go to a specialised site such as www.caninefreestyle.co.uk.

Conformation Shows

Over the past decade, many people who have never been to a canine sporting event in person have nevertheless watched Crufts, on television. In this type of show, the dog is judged against his breed standard to see how well he conforms to that measure of excellence. Traditionally, dog shows were meant to give breeders an opportunity to see how potential breeding animals stacked up to others of their breed.

Dog shows (conformation events) are intended to evaluate breeding stock. Therefore, only sexually intact dogs qualify for conventional Kennel Club conformation events. The size of these events ranges from large all-breed shows, with huge entries to small club shows featuring a specific breed. The dog's overall appearance and structure, or conformation—often an indication of the dog's ability to produce quality puppies—is judged.

There are three types of conformation dog shows, as follows:

- All-breed shows offer competitions for over 150 breeds and varieties of dogs recognised by the Kennel Club. Crufts is the premier all-breed show in the UK, and it is an annual fixture.
- Shows restricted to dogs of a specific breed or to varieties of one breed.
- Group shows are limited to dogs belonging to one of the seven KC groups. Russells compete in the Terrier Group.

Numerous opportunities to show your Russell to his championship title abound. Like flea markets and horse shows, you can find one nearly every weekend of the year—holidays included. There are lots of rosettes on offer at every show, and winning Best of Breed is a great honour. If you're not careful, dog showing can become an addiction!

If your dog is show quality, your Russell's breeder or knowledgeable members of a breed club will honestly help you assess his chances of attaining his Championship. Showing a dog, however, is hardly as easy as it appears. That's the paradox: It requires a lot of skill to make it look easy. Training your dog to "stack" (pose properly), to stand still while being examined, and to "show his heart out" requires practice. It takes more than good conformation and flashy movement to make a winner. It's that hypnotic je ne sais quoi that tells the judge, "You will pick me!" Many gorgeous dogs simply lack the necessary attitude to achieve the top levels or even finish a championship. A beautiful dog with the personality of tapioca pudding is unlikely to win shows.

For most people, that top level is a Kennel Club Championship. To become a Champion, a dog must win three Challenge Certificates (CCs) under three different judges. Judges examine the dogs and then give awards according to how closely each dog compares to their mental image of the "perfect" dog as described in the breed's official standard.
A dog show is really an elimination contest. Male dogs compete against males (called "dogs") and females against females (called "bitches"—their proper appellation) in each breed, with the best of each sex being awarded a Challenge Certificate.

This dog has a distinctive face, but it's how well he conforms to his breed standard overall that will earn him points in conformation showing.

The rules and procedures for earning championships are quite different in the different registries, so be sure to obtain the rulebooks, and if possible, observe a show or two before entering. Your dog must, of course, be registered with the organisation that sanctions the show.

If you think you'd like to try showing in conformation, and you don't yet own a dog, explain your desires to breeders. Most breeders won't entrust a truly outstanding pup to a beginner, but many breeders will sell you a good-quality dog with the potential to finish the championship. You can learn with that dog and find out if you like showing. As we've already seen, responsible breeders are cautious when placing sexually intact pups, so you may be required to keep the breeder's name on the dog's registration papers as co-owner until you prove yourself. There may be other strings attached as well, so be sure you understand the terms of purchase on your show prospect, and be sure you're comfortable with them.

Sometimes people already have a dog when they become interested in showing. If that's true for you, try not to let your love for your dog blind you to his shortcomings. Your dog may be a once-in-a-lifetime companion and the most beautiful canine in the world to you, but that doesn't necessarily make him show quality. It's important to be as aware of your dog's faults as you are of his virtues. Every dog has traits that could be closer to the ideal for the breed, and if he has a lot of faults or a single serious or fault, he won't be able to compete successfully.

In conformation showing, your terrier will be judged against the standard for the breed.

Try to enlist the help of someone who knows the breed well—a breeder or show judge if possible—to evaluate your dog and explain her observations to you. Your dog's own breeder may be a good choice if she shows her dogs. Sometimes breeders place show-quality dogs as pets because they consider a good home more important than titles, and sometimes a pup turns out better than the breeder predicted when the pup was eight weeks old. But your puppy may have been placed as a pet because he has faults that make him unsuitable for showing or breeding. If your dog's breeder doesn't think the dog should be shown, please honour her opinion. Remember, her name will appear in show catalogues as your dog's breeder, and your dog will represent her breeding programme and her judgment to the world. If the dog you have isn't a show dog, love him and train and participate with him in other activities. If you still want to show in conformation, you will need to buy a show prospect.

If your terrier does seem to have potential as a

show dog, you both need to train. Helping a dog look terrific in the conformation ring is harder than it looks, and nothing will hurt your dog's chances of winning more than being untrained and poorly presented. Go to shows and watch the handlers carefully. Observe how the good ones make their dogs stand out in the ring. If there's a ringcraft class in your area, sign up. Local clubs sometimes sponsor seminars by professional handlers, and you can learn a lot in a short time at a good seminar. Learn to groom your terrier properly for the show ring as well. Read books and magazine and web articles on show handling. If possible, attend a few shows with an experienced exhibitor or your dog's breeder before you enter.

Dog showing is one of few sports in which you can enter nearly any event with no experience at all. Still, I suggest that you start with a small, limited show. In some cases you may be competing against dogs of different breeds, but it is all good experience and can be very enjoyable. The two of you can practice without the pressures of a real show.

Remember that a dog show is a show, and the way you present yourself and your dog affects your success. In theory, dogs are judged strictly on their merits as representatives of their breeds. Realistically, your terrier's grooming, your appearance, your dog's performance as he moves, stands, and is examined, and your handling ability all contribute to your success in the show ring. Dress for the occasion. Men conventionally wear smart trousers, shirt and tie, and a sports jacket. Women can wear trousers or a skirt with a nice blouse, sweater, or jacket, or a dress. Wear safe, comfortable shoes that suit the rest of your outfit. Avoid anything that flops around, including jewellery, scarves, unclipped ties, and billowy skirts. Solid colours or reasonably subdued patterns work best. Check yourself out in a mirror, preferably alongside your dog, before you enter the ring. You want all eyes on your dog, not on you, whether because you're a fashion plate or a fashion faux-pas.

Whether you participate in dog sports just for fun, to earn titles, or to strive for high-level awards and honours, the time you spend will help channel some of that terrier enthusiasm into safe, nondestructive, and even productive activity. Most important, it will enhance the bond you have with your dog. Win or lose, never forget that it wasn't ribbons and titles that brought you there first—it was your love for a dog.

Dress for Success

If you get bitten by the dog show bug and decide that this activity is for you, remember that it's not just your dog who is making an impression in the ring. While his appearance needs to be as perfect as possible, you need to look your best, too, and be sure that what you wear isn't detracting from the judge's attention on your dog.

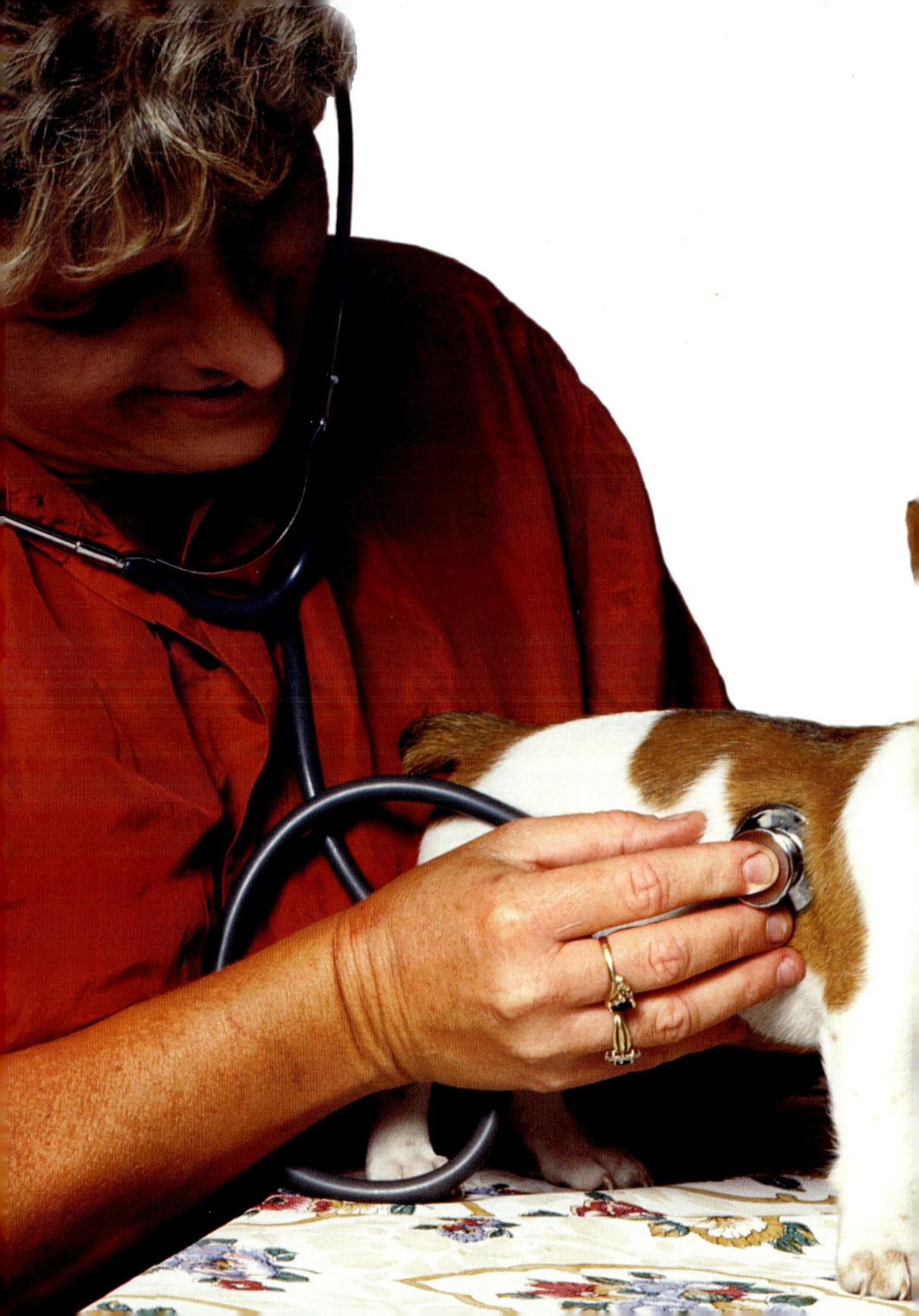

8

HEALTH

of Your Parson or Jack Russell Terrier

A carefully bred Parson Russell or Jack Russell Terrier is generally a healthy, hardy dog, but like all animals, he can become ill or injured. Some health problems, including injuries and contagious diseases, can be acquired from the environment. Other health problems are inherited, or passed from parent to puppy in the genes. A few health problems require both an inherited predisposition for the problem and an environmental event to trigger it.

In this chapter, we'll discuss some of the things you can do to keep your Russell healthy through good veterinary and home care. Then we'll take a look at some of the health problems seen most commonly in the breed. Even though most Russells are healthy, a buyer or owner who is forewarned has an advantage when it comes to having a healthy dog.

ROUTINE VETERINARY CARE FOR YOUR TERRIER

Finding the Right Vet

Your veterinary surgeon is as important to your dog's well-being as your own doctor is to yours. You should feel confident in your vet's knowledge and skills, and you should be comfortable asking questions and making your own opinions and wishes known. The vet closest to your home may not be your best choice. It's worth a small investment of time to find the right practice and individual vet for the life of your dog.

You can find a vet in the phonebook or online, but recommendations from other dog owners are a better source of information. If you purchased your dog from a local breeder or rescue programme, they can suggest someone. Other good sources of information are your obedience instructor, members of local dog clubs, and friends who have dogs, especially terriers. Ask people what vets they use and what they like and don't like about their vets and the practices in which they work.

When you have narrowed down the possibilities, ask for a tour of the practice and a brief meeting with the vet you are considering. Don't wait until you have a doggy emergency. Many vets won't charge anything for a visit of this type, but even if they do, it's worth the cost of a surgery call to be sure you're comfortable putting your dog's health care—in fact, his life—in the hands of this person. If you're interested in alternative therapies, newer vaccination protocols, or other non-traditional approaches to canine health care, find a vet whose ideas are compatible with yours. As in all areas of life, there are many competent, caring vets and there are other vets with poor skills and poor attitudes. For your dog's sake as well as your own, take the time to find a good vet.

During your dog's first check-up, the vet will check his general health and condition and establish baselines for future reference.

Your Terrier's First Check-up

Your new puppy or dog should have a check-up with your vet within a day or two of coming home, even if he was examined recently by his breeder's or rescuer's vet. This initial examination will allow your vet to check your terrier's general health and condition and establish baselines for future reference. Your vet will examine your dog's skin and coat, ears, gums, bite, and external eye area. She will also listen to his heart and lungs, and she should check his knees for luxating patellas (knee caps that slip out of position) and flex his other joints to check for range of motion and any signs of discomfort. If your puppy or dog has a record of previous vaccinations, take that along—there's no point in giving him vaccinations he doesn't need. You may need to take a faecal sample so that your vet can check it for internal parasites.

This first visit to the vet is just the beginning. Good regular veterinary care, including at least an annual check-up and preventive care, will help your terrier live a longer, healthier life.

Vaccinations

Like human babies, puppies are most vulnerable to infectious diseases during their first few months of life. Newborn puppies born to a healthy, properly vaccinated bitch receive some immunity from colostrum, an antibody-rich substance produced by the dam's teats during the first few days after birth. Unfortunately, the protection a puppy receives from colostrum doesn't last long, and sometime between the fifth and tenth weeks the pup's immunity wears off. That's why your puppy needs vaccinations to stimulate his immune system to fight off disease.

Most vaccines are given by subcutaneous (under the skin) or intramuscular (into the muscle) injection, but a few are given in nasal sprays. Traditionally, puppies are given a series of vaccinations beginning at 5 to 8 weeks of age and ending at about 16 weeks, followed by annual boosters. In recent years, however, concerns have been raised that excessive vaccination can damage the immune system and cause serious long-term health problems. Because of these concerns, some vets now don't begin puppy vaccinations until 10 to 12 weeks of age, followed by monthly vaccinations until the series is complete. Some vets believe those vaccines are effective for the life of the dog, while others recommend booster vaccinations one year after the puppy series and then every three years. (The exception is rabies vaccinations, in countries where this is applicable.)

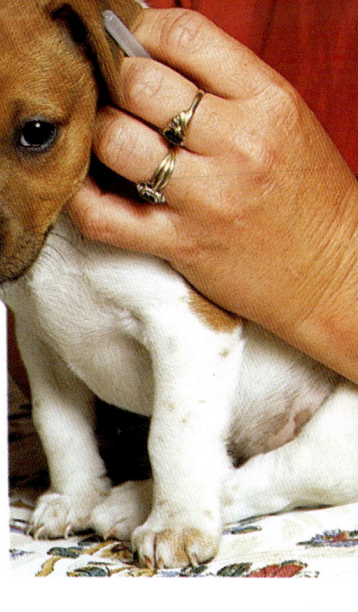

Vaccinations help protect puppies from a variety of diseases.

Sometimes the booster shots are staggered so that each is given about every three years, but only one or two are given each year. Rather than giving automatic booster shots, some vets recommend checking immunity levels with antibody titers (blood tests that check for antibodies to specific diseases) every year and boosting the vaccine if necessary, but others don't believe that titers are reliable.

Dogs are commonly vaccinated against some or all of the following diseases.

Rabies

Rabies is a deadly viral disease of the central nervous system. When most people picture a rabid animal, they imagine one affected with furious rabies, a form of the disease in which the animal foams at the mouth and becomes insanely aggressive. But another form of the disease, known as dumb rabies, also occurs. An animal with dumb rabies becomes paralysed, first in the lower jaw, then the limbs, and eventually the vital organs. Once the symptoms of rabies appear, the disease is always fatal.

Rabies, which can attack any warm-blooded animal, is spread in the saliva of infected animals. It is widespread in North America and some other areas of the world, but it is not present in the UK. However, if you plan to travel with your dog, he will need to be fully vaccinated against rabies. Domestic animals commonly acquire rabies from wild animals. In the US, dogs and cats must be vaccinated against rabies at regular intervals. Some require yearly vaccinations, while others require vaccinations every three years. A puppy should have his first rabies vaccination at approximately four months of age and then receive boosters as required.

Canine Distemper

Canine distemper is a highly contagious viral disease that causes respiratory difficulties, vomiting, diarrhoea, and problems of the nervous system. It kills most of the puppies and about half of the adult dogs it infects. Survivors are often partly or completely paralysed, and some suffer full or partial loss of their vision, hearing, and sense of smell. There are no effective antiviral drugs for canine distemper, so the best that can be done for a dog with the disease is to treat the symptoms.

The distemper virus attacks the linings of the lungs and intestines, so antibiotics are usually given to fight off bacteria that might further damage the organs. Other medications are given to protect the intestines and treat diarrhoea, and electrolyte fluids are given intravenously to prevent dehydration. Vitamins and other essential nutrients are often administered by injection to keep up the dog's strength while he is unable to eat normally. Puppies normally receive two vaccinations against distemper, but practices may vary.

Infectious Canine Hepatitis

Infectious canine hepatitis is a viral disease spread in the urine of infected dogs. The disease can attack many tissues and organs but usually causes the most damage to the liver. Puppies are normally given two vaccinations. Mild cases usually run their course in a week or two, during which time the dog will likely be depressed, lose his appetite, and have a slightly elevated temperature. Sometimes the cornea of the eye will turn bluish a week or two after onset of the disease. Coughing, discharge from

Terminology

The correct name for a canine female is bitch, while the term dog denotes a male. A young female, then, is a puppy bitch, and a young male is a puppy dog. The dam (not dame!) is the mother, and the sire (not sir!) is the father.

the nose and eyes, and respiratory problems occur in some dogs, making the disease easy to mistake for bordetellosis (kennel cough). In puppies and some older dogs, the disease can be much more serious, causing abdominal pain, diarrhoea, vomiting, edema (swelling from fluid in the tissues), and sometimes jaundice. Severe cases are often fatal. Treatment for infectious canine hepatitis usually involves antibiotics to prevent secondary infections as the virus weakens the body. Intravenous fluids are often given to prevent dehydration.

Canine Parvovirus

Canine parvovirus (CPV), or "parvo," is a viral disease that attacks the intestinal tract, heart muscle, and white blood cells, causing vomiting, severe and distinctively foul-smelling diarrhoea, depression, high fever, and loss of appetite. Treatment is intensive and expensive, because hospitalisation and close monitoring are required. Fluids are given intravenously to prevent dehydration, and drugs are given to control diarrhoea and vomiting. Antibiotics are also administered to prevent secondary infections, and additional therapies may be recommended depending on the particular case. Many dogs die within two or three days of showing initial symptoms. Puppies less than 12 weeks old who survive an attack of parvo often suffer permanent heart damage from myocarditis (inflammation of the heart).

Lethargy, depression, and appetite loss may be signs of a serious health problem.

The virus that causes parvo is passed in the faeces of infected dogs and is easily spread from place to place on shoes, paws, and clothing. It's very difficult to eradicate, surviving most disinfectants and extreme temperatures, so once introduced to an area, parvo remains a threat for a long time. Puppies are generally given two vaccinations for parvovirus.

Canine Bordetellosis

Canine bordetellosis (also known as bordetella or kennel cough) is a bacterial disease of the respiratory tract. Kennel cough usually isn't very serious in an otherwise healthy adult, but it can kill a puppy or elderly dog. Symptoms are rather like a bad cold, with copious nasal discharge and a horrendous cough. Antibiotics are sometimes given to dogs with kennel cough, but the disease usually runs its course in a few days in healthy dogs. Bordetella vaccines are usually given in nasal sprays, but injectable vaccines are also available.

Canine Parainfluenza

Canine parainfluenza is an infection of the respiratory tract caused by a virus. The primary symptom is a cough, more severe after the dog has exercised or is excited, which may be labelled "kennel cough," although that term is more commonly applied to bordetella. In an otherwise healthy adult dog, the disease usually runs its course in five to ten days, but it can weaken the immune system enough to let secondary bacterial infections take hold, so antibiotics are sometimes given. Puppies usually receive two vaccinations, often in combination with other vaccines.

Because there are all sorts of organisms that can cause your dog to be ill, it's important to immunise him against the most serious diseases.

Canine Leptospirosis

Canine leptospirosis, or "lepto," is caused by bacteria that attack the kidneys and/or liver. Lepto, which is spread in the urine of infected animals, is rare in most areas. Symptoms include vomiting, convulsions, vision problems, depression, loss of appetite, and fever. The disease appears in several different strains, and unfortunately, the vaccine has little effect on the most common strain. Because serious reactions to the vaccine are not uncommon, many vets and owners choose not to vaccinate against lepto, especially if the risk of exposure is low for their dogs. If you think your dog is at risk of contracting lepto, consider having the vaccine given at a different time from the others and stay at the surgery for half an hour or so after the vaccination is given in case of a negative reaction.

Coronavirus

Coronavirus is a viral disease that attacks the lining of the small intestine. Vaccination is recommended solely in areas where the disease is rampant. Initial symptoms include depression, loss of appetite, and lethargy, followed by vomiting (sometimes with blood in the vomit) and projectile diarrhoea.

Lyme Disease

Lyme disease is a bacterial disease spread by the bite of an infected tick, most commonly the tiny deer tick. The disease, which causes pain in multiple joints due to arthritic changes is rare in the UK, but becoming more common. Early symptoms, which typically appear about two months after exposure, may include lethargy, loss of appetite, and fever, followed by lameness. Treatment usually includes antibiotics and analgesics for the arthritis. Prognosis for recovery depends on how severe the case is and how soon it is diagnosed. A vaccine is available, but it is not necessary for all dogs. Talk to your vet to see if your dog should be vaccinated for Lyme disease.

The Lyme Vaccine

Lyme disease is a tick-borne illness that can seriously debilitate your dog. Talk to your vet about vaccinating against the disease. If you live in an area where Lyme is prevalent, it may be a worthwhile option for you.

SHOULD YOU BREED YOUR TERRIER?

You love your dog, and puppies are so cute that you may be tempted to breed a litter. No doubt, there are good reasons to breed good dogs. However, there are even more good reasons not to breed most dogs. Let's look at the realities of dog breeding and at the advantages of neutering your pet so that you can make an intelligent decision.

The Realities of Dog Breeding

With the large number of homeless dogs already in the world, the only good reason to breed dogs is to produce puppies who combine the very best characteristics of their breeds and who have as few of the undesirable characteristics as possible. Love and good intentions won't produce healthy dogs with proper temperaments—responsible breeding also requires knowledge, careful planning, time, and money.

Because puppies inherit both bad and good traits from their parents, responsible breeders use science and careful pedigree research to increase the chances that their puppies will inherit desirable traits. Screening tests for genetic diseases are expensive, and research to learn as much as possible about the dogs' ancestors takes a lot of time, but breeding without these tools increases the odds that your dog will have puppies with serious problems. Before you breed your bitch, she needs at least to have her eyes examined by a veterinary ophthalmologist. She should also be screened for luxating patellas, Legg-Perthes disease, von Willebrand's disease, and heart problems, and you will want to research the history of these diseases as well as epilepsy and cerebellar ataxia in her close relatives. Even if she hasn't yet shown signs of having those diseases herself, she may carry the genes and pass them on to her puppies.

It's also a good idea to have someone who really knows Parson or Jack Russell Terriers evaluate your bitch to see how closely she conforms to the appropriate breed standard. Don't depend on your vet to do this (unless she's an expert on the breed); many vets don't know much about good breeding practices or about individual breeds. If the evaluator points out faults in your bitch, keep an open mind. If your bitch has a serious fault, which would seriously affect her chances in the show ring, or if she doesn't pass the health screening tests, then breeding her is almost guaranteed to produce puppies with problems. Even if she has no big problems, knowing where she needs improvement will help you

Breeding is a very big responsibility that should be undertaken only by those people who are completely committed to bettering the breed.

choose a stud dog who is strong where she is weak, so that the puppies will (hopefully) be better than both parents. Even if your puppies will be pets, you'll want them to be good-looking, healthy terriers their owners can live with and be proud of. All of these also apply if you own a male Parson or Jack Russell Terrier and want to stand him at stud, of course.

Pregnancy and Whelping

If you decide to go ahead and breed a litter, you will need to see your bitch through nearly nine weeks of pregnancy and another seven weeks or longer of caring for a litter of puppies. Puppies need a safe environment, room to play, toys, food beginning in about their fourth week, veterinary care, and many hours of gentle handling and socialisation. Puppies pee and poop, throw up, spill food and water, tear and break things, and dig holes, so you'll need plenty of cleaning supplies and patience. Puppies also can be injured or become ill and require special veterinary care in addition to routine examinations and vaccinations. This is if all goes well.

You are responsible for all the puppies your female produces, from the moment of their birth to their lifetime care.

Unfortunately, pregnancies and puppies don't always go well. A number of health problems can affect a pregnant bitch, including gestational diabetes, which can threaten the lives of both the mother and the pups. In addition, puppies can die in utero, causing a life-threatening infection in the bitch, and bitches can die giving birth. Puppies can also die in the birthing process.

Whelping—the birthing of puppies—often occurs in the middle of the night or other inconvenient times, and delivery can take a long, long time. Worse yet, what if things go terribly wrong? Are you prepared, emotionally, physically, and financially, to take your bitch for an emergency Caesarean in the middle of the night? Can you face the possibility of losing your beloved pet or her puppies, or all of them together? Could you handle the birth of a puppy with a serious birth defect such as a cleft palate that prevents him from nursing properly, deformed or missing organs, hydrocephalus, or other serious problems? Can you face the possibility of having a puppy die in your hands in spite of your best efforts to keep him alive? These are some of the hazards on the breeder's path, and for many people they take all the pleasure out of breeding puppies.

Even if your bitch has no problems and her puppies are all healthy, that's not the end of the story. All of those friends and relatives who wanted puppies a few months ago have a funny way of disappearing just when the pups are ready for homes. You are responsible for every puppy you cause to be born, even if it's inconvenient. Are you willing to take care of every puppy for as long as necessary and to accept back any pups whose new homes don't work out? Not all puppies find loving, responsible homes—visit your local rescue centre and you'll see. Many beautiful, healthy puppies die every day in shelters for no reason except that they have no homes. Don't let them be your puppies.

Many breeders are dedicated to producing fine terriers despite the risks and responsibilities, but far too many people breed their pets without considering the whole picture. Responsible dog breeding is physically and mentally exhausting, expensive, time consuming, and at times, tragic. When things go wrong, it's the puppies and their buyers who suffer. Having your dog neutered will make both of you happier.

Neutering (Spaying and Castrating)

Most responsible breeders and vets encourage owners to neuter all but the very best individuals in terms of breed type, temperament, and individual and inherited health. If you get a rescued dog, it will be neutered before rehoming. It is now acknowledged by all canine experts that neutering is the best policy for all pet dogs.

Why the big fuss? Visit your local rescue centre, or call a terrier rescue organisation, and you'll soon realise that many, many Parson Russell and Jack Russell Terriers and other wonderful dogs lose their homes each year. Many of them are eventually euthanised because of a shortage of homes.

Responsible dog ownership includes a commitment

to the welfare of any puppies your pet produces. That means that your terrier shouldn't give birth to or sire a single puppy unless you are willing to care for that puppy throughout his life if necessary.

Pet overpopulation isn't the only reason to neuter your pet. Spaying (removal of the ovaries and uterus) eliminates the risks of pregnancy and whelping, prevents life-threatening cancers or infections of the uterus and ovaries, and if done before she has her first heat or at least before she's two years old, greatly reduces your pet's risk of developing mammary tumours later in life. Spaying also makes a bitch easier to live with, because she doesn't experience the hormonal swings of an intact bitch, nor will she attract canine Casanovas to your door.

Some people have the mistaken idea that having a litter will calm a bitch down and make her sweeter and more loving. But the truth is that training, exercise, and maturity lead to calmer behaviour, not motherhood. Having puppies will focus your pet's attention away from her human family, and she may become very protective of her puppies. Even when she doesn't have puppies, fluctuating hormone levels can make an unspayed bitch moody and sometimes aggressive, especially with other bitches. Spaying makes for a more emotionally stable pet.

Castration will not only keep your male dog from siring puppies, with or without your permission, but it will also minimise some of the behaviours that people find annoying in stud dogs, including territorial urine marking and roaming in search of females. An unneutered male dog is a mess when he detects a bitch in heat—which he can do from miles away! He will refuse to eat, whine, pace the floor, howl, and slobber. He'll be distracted and may get pretty pushy. Neutering won't make your dog wimpy, but it will probably make him more tolerant of other male dogs and less interested in picking fights. Castration also offers health benefits, such as the prevention of testicular cancer and a reduction of the risk of prostate problems.

Neutering won't change your terrier's basic personality. On the

Dogs who have been neutered can be expected to behave more consistently.

contrary, it will eliminate the urges brought on by sex hormones and let the positive aspects of your pet's personality shine. Neutering won't make your dog fat, either; eating too much and getting too little exercise are the main causes of obesity.

PARASITES

Parasites attack all animals, and your terrier is a potential host for a wide range of parasites that live in or on his body. Some parasites inflict little or no harm on their hosts, but others do. Fortunately, there are now effective ways to prevent or control most common parasites that attack dogs.

External Parasites

External parasites, including fleas, ticks, and mites, live on your dog's skin. They are more than disgusting and annoying—they spread disease, and their bites can become infected or cause allergic reactions in some dogs. Knowledge is power, though, so work with your vet to protect your dog (and yourself) from these little monsters.

Fleas

Thoroughly inspect your Russell for fleas and ticks after he has been playing outdoors.

Most dog owners will encounter a flea or two sometime in their dogs' lives. Fleas are tiny red, black, or brown hard-shelled insects that suck and eat blood from their hosts. Flea larvae eat the adult fleas' blood-rich faeces, or "flea dirt," which looks rather like black pepper on the animal's skin. Because it's mostly blood, if you wet it slightly, flea dirt turns red.

Fleas lay their eggs in grass, carpets, rugs, or bedding and

occasionally directly on the host animal. Under normal conditions, the eggs hatch in 4 to 21 days, but they can survive for months before hatching. The larvae look like tiny maggots. Flea larvae moult twice, then form a pupa that can survive long periods until temperature or vibration from a nearby host stimulates the adult fleas to emerge.

Fleas are annoying, no doubt, but they also pose serious health threats to their hosts, who can include people. They spread disease and tapeworm larvae. In large numbers, they can consume enough blood to cause anaemia. A dog who is allergic to flea saliva may scratch himself raw from even a single flea bite, opening the way to infection.

If you find fleas on your dog or in your home or garden, speak to your vet about the best flea-control options for your situation. Over-the-counter flea controls are not the most effective or cost effective, and they can even be dangerous, so you're better off using a higher quality product. For treatment to work, you will need to treat all your pets as well as their environment.

Staying Flea Free
Proper nutrition and overall good health will help your dog be less attractive to fleas, but these pests are persistent. The best preventive is your attention. Check for fleas regularly, and as soon as you spot any, alert your vet and use products that will rid your dog and your home of fleas as quickly and safely as possible.

Ticks

Your terrier may pick up ticks in tall grass, undergrowth, or wooded areas, and animals and birds can carry ticks into your garden and home. Ticks are small arthropods (relatives of spiders). They have eight legs, and their bodies are round and flat unless they are engorged with a meal of blood or gravid with eggs, in which case they look like beans with legs.

A hungry tick buries its head parts in the host's flesh and gorges on blood. Ticks, like fleas, carry diseases, including Rocky Mountain spotted fever and ehrlichia, so control and careful removal are important. A fine-toothed flea comb works well for detecting ticks. When removing a tick, it's important not to squeeze disease-bearing fluid from the tick into the host, or to pull the tick's head off in the host's skin, which can cause an infection. To remove a tick safely, first dab it with a strong saline solution, iodine, or alcohol to make it loosen its grip. Then, gently pull straight out using a tick remover (available from pet shops) or using forceps, tweezers, or your fingers. (Wear rubber gloves for protection.) Check the skin; you should see a small hole where the tick bit your dog. If you see a black spot, you may have left the head, in

If your dogs go everywhere with you, you'll want to know that they're protected against parasites.

which case you will need to keep a close eye on the site for several days in case it becomes infected. Clean the site with alcohol or an antibacterial cleanser, dry it, and apply antiseptic ointment. Wash your hands and tools with soap and hot water.

The tiny little deer tick is a threat in some areas because it spreads Lyme disease, which can cripple a dog (or a person). Deer ticks are often not noticeable until after they have been feeding on the host for several days, and by then they've injected the Lyme bacteria into the host. Lyme disease is still rare in the UK, but its incidence is increasing. Ask your vet about the danger of Lyme disease where you live or travel, and check to see whether you should vaccinate your dog. If you walk your dog in tick-infested areas, check your dog and yourself carefully afterwards. Ticks don't usually attach to the host for several hours, so you may be able to catch them before a bite occurs. If ticks are a problem where you live, talk to your vet about an effective prevention programme.

Mites

Mites are microscopic arachnids that can cause a variety of diseases in dogs. One such disease, mange, is caused by any of several species of tiny mites that eat skin debris, hair follicles, and tissue. Dogs with mange typically lose hair and have crusty patches of irritated skin. Severe itching often causes them to scratch themselves raw, making it easy for viral, fungal, or parasitic infections to occur. Some forms of mange are contagious; others are not. Home remedies are usually ineffective and may make matters worse, so if you think your dog might have mange, see your vet. She will take a skin scraping and examine it under a microscope for mites, determine the species that is attacking your dog, and then prescribe an appropriate treatment programme for the affected dog and a prevention programme for your other pets.

Internal Parasites

Your dog, like all animals, is a potential host for several species of parasitic internal worms. Some worms affect the host animal's health very little, but others can cause illness, and some can kill. When your puppy gets his vaccinations, your vet should perform a microscopic examination of your puppy's faeces to check for evidence of parasites, and as an adult, your dog should have a faecal examination at least once a year. Of course, if you see signs of worms in your dog's stools or around his anus at other times, take a specimen to your vet—earlier treatment is better than later.

Heartworm

The heartworm is a parasitic worm that lives in the host's heart. It is rarely found in the UK. When a mosquito bites a dog infected with heartworms, it ingests the microscopic heartworm larvae and subsequently transmits the larvae when it bites another dog. The larvae travel through the blood vessels to the host's heart, where they mature and reproduce. When enough heartworms are present, they clog the vessels and cause congestive heart failure.

Talk to your vet about how old your puppy should be when he begins taking monthly heartworm preventive.

Heartworm disease causes no symptoms until a large number of worms infest the heart. At that advanced stage of the disease, the dog will have symptoms of congestive heart failure, including coughing (especially after exercise), difficulty breathing, and low energy levels. His coat will become dull, and his abdomen may become enlarged. By the time the disease has advanced this far, it may be too late for effective treatment, so prevention is essential.

Heartworm disease is a problem in some places and practically unheard of in others. Ask your vet about the risk of heartworm disease where you live and travel with your dog. Luckily, heartworm disease is easy to prevent with a variety of medications. If you live in an area where heartworm is a problem, your dog should be kept on a heartworm prevention programme throughout his life. It's important to realise, though, that even the best prevention is

Worms Away

A clean environment, keeping up with regular veterinary visits, and limiting your dog's exposure to places where worms may be festering — such as areas where many other animals congregate — are all ways to safeguard your dog against an invasion by internal parasites.

not 100 percent effective. Early diagnosis and treatment are essential, so all dogs should be checked every year or two for the presence of heartworm larvae in the blood.

Ringworm

Ringworm is not a worm but a highly contagious fungus that spreads easily among animals and people. Typically, ringworm appears as a raw-looking bald circle, but sometimes bald patches appear without the rawness. Like many fungal infections, ringworm is difficult to treat effectively. If you find any sort of bald spot on your dog, take him to the vet for proper diagnosis and treatment and instructions for preventing the spread of the disease. Don't wait to see if it gets better or fool around with home remedies; if you do, you may end up with a much bigger problem.

Roundworm

Roundworms are very common parasites in puppies and adult dogs. Even puppies from responsible breeders with clean facilities and healthy dogs often have roundworms, because if the mother has ever had roundworms, she may have roundworm larvae encysted in her body, and she can pass the larvae to her pup through her milk even though examination will not reveal that she's infected. Puppies may also pick up roundworm eggs from the ground, where the eggs are deposited by a wide variety of other animals, including earthworms, beetles, rodents, poultry, and other dogs.

Roundworms look like strings of spaghetti and can be up to 8 inches (20 cm) long. They eat food that is being digested in the host's intestines. At first, an infected puppy will seem ravenous all the time, but eventually he'll become so weak from malnutrition that he'll stop eating. A puppy with a massive or chronic infection will develop a potbelly and will vomit and have diarrhoea.

Fortunately, roundworms are easy to eliminate with the proper medication. People can get roundworms, too, so it's important for everyone who has contact with an infected puppy or dog to practice careful hygiene until the vet declares your puppy free of worms.

Tapeworm

Tapeworms, which can grow to be several feet long, also eat food digesting in the host's intestine. To complete its life cycle, the tapeworm requires two different hosts. In the larval stage, the tapeworm inhabits an intermediate host such as a mouse, rabbit, or flea. If your dog ingests an infected animal, the larvae move to his intestines and develop into adult tapeworms. Tapeworms usually do not show up in faecal specimens but are diagnosed by the appearance of rice-like segments that break off the worm and stick to the tissue and hair around the dog's anus. If your terrier kills and eats wild animals, or if he has had fleas, watch for tapeworm evidence. If you think your dog may be infected, talk to your vet. Effective wormers will solve the problem.

Other Internal Parasites

Puppies and dogs can also be hosts to other parasites, including hookworms, whipworms, threadworms, coccidia, and giardia. The effects vary but may include weight loss, anaemia, respiratory infection, and diarrhoea. Fortunately, a clean environment, close observation, and regular examinations by your vet will help protect your dog from parasites.

Some dogs suffer from food allergies, which can cause itching, difficulty breathing, excessive licking, and a variety of other symptoms.

HEALTH ISSUES IN PARSON RUSSELL AND JACK RUSSELL TERRIERS

Compared to some breeds of dogs, Parson Russell and Jack Russell Terriers enjoy excellent health. Nevertheless, like all dogs, purebred and mixed, they can suffer a variety of health problems. Knowledge is the best weapon you have for defending your dog against illness, so let's look at the more common health challenges for Parson Russell and Jack Russell Terriers.

Allergies

Allergies are fairly common in dogs, and they can have a wide range of causes. Some of the most common include moulds, pollen and other plant matter, dust mites, insect bites (including flea

A sufficient amount of exercise will help keep your Russell healthier.

bites), and food ingredients.

Inhalant allergens (those that the dog inhales) typically cause itchy, oily, irritated skin, which the dog scratches, chews, licks, and bites. Food allergies also cause itching, head shaking, face rubbing, inflammation of the ears, excessive licking (especially of the front paws), diarrhoea and/or vomiting, flatulence, sneezing, breathing problems, and sometimes behavioural changes or seizures.

If your terrier is scratching or licking himself a lot, take him to the vet. The faster you can stop the scratching, the better chance you have of preventing open sores, which can be very hard to clear up. If the problem persists, consider seeing a veterinary dermatologist; the extra cost will pay off in more effective treatment, which will save you money in the long run and save your dog a lot of misery. When searching for the cause of an allergy, keep an open mind—sensitivities to allergens can develop after long-term, seemingly problem-free exposure.

A variety of treatments are used for dogs with allergies. If possible, remove the source of the allergy. Antihistamines are safe for most dogs and effective for some. Check with your vet concerning dosage and potential interaction with any other drugs your dog is taking. Corticosteroids are sometimes used in extreme cases on a short-term basis to reduce inflammation and the itching it causes, but they can have serious side effects. As a result, they are normally used only for short-term control of allergy symptoms. Fatty acids (omega-3 and omega-6) help some dogs, but they take three to four weeks to have any effect, and they don't stop the itching. Immunotherapy (allergy injections) is safe and effective, but it requires testing to determine the allergens causing the problem and may take up to a year to become effective. Always check with your vet before beginning any course of treatment.

Allergies

People are plagued by allergies, and dogs can be, too. If your terrier is licking or scratching excessively, suspect allergies and consult your vet. You may be able to eliminate a particular allergen, or you may need to begin a therapeutic treatment.

Brain and Nervous System Disorders

The canine brain and nervous system are complex and delicate and are potentially subject to inherited and acquired problems. Let's look at the most common ones.

Seizures

Seizures, sometimes called "fits," can have many non-hereditary causes, including physical trauma to the head, chemicals, medications, disease, and heatstroke, among others. If a dog suffers seizures due to environmental influences such as drugs or chemicals, removing the cause will usually stop them. If head trauma is the cause, antiseizure medication may control the seizures so that the dog can live a reasonably normal life.

Epilepsy

Epilepsy is a seizure disorder that occurs in most breeds of dogs and in mixed breeds. True, or primary (also known as idiopathic), epilepsy is inherited. Epilepsy cannot be cured, but it can often be controlled with medication. Most epileptic dogs can live fairly normal lives, but under no circumstances should a dog with epilepsy be bred from. Before you buy a puppy, ask the breeder about epilepsy in the dog's bloodlines. One relative with seizures is not necessarily cause for concern, but beware if your dog has multiple close relatives with the disease.

Cerebellar Ataxia

Cerebellar ataxia refers to lack of balance (ataxia) linked to problems in the cerebellum, the part of the brain that controls balance. Some non-inherited, environmental factors that can cause loss of balance include head trauma, toxins, and disease. Parson Russell and Jack Russell Terriers and some other breeds are also

Most Parson and Jack Russell Terriers enjoy excellent health.

subject to inherited cerebellar ataxia, a condition caused by premature death of certain cells in the cerebellum. The disease is progressive (meaning it gets worse over time), and affected puppies can show symptoms of ataxia as soon as they start walking (around two to three weeks of age).

Typically, a puppy with cerebellar ataxia will bob his head, shake, have trouble standing or stand with his feet wide apart, and "goose step" when trying to walk. Some pups become unable to stand at all by seven weeks of age, while others are able to walk with difficulty. Although some affected dogs live for years, they require considerable extra care. Both parents must carry the gene in order for a puppy to have the disease, and researchers are working to identify the genetic marker for cerebellar ataxia so that carriers can be identified before they produce affected puppies.

Spinocerebellar Ataxia

Spinocerebellar ataxia is similar to cerebellar ataxia, but it shows up later—typically when the dog is about five months old—and is not as debilitating.

Myasthenia Gravis

Myasthenia gravis is a neuromuscular disease in which certain nerve receptors fail to function properly, blocking the ability of muscles to contract. It may affect only a few muscles, or it may practically immobilise the dog. Tests can confirm suspected cases, and with proper diagnosis and treatment, dogs can live a long time with the disease.

Cancer

Cancers affect dogs of all kinds. Cancers can attack any part of the body and may progress very slowly or very quickly. Early diagnosis greatly improves the chances for successful treatment, which may include surgery, radiation, and chemotherapy. Let's look at some of the most common cancers in dogs.

Lymphosarcoma

Lymphosarcoma is a common, very aggressive cancer of lymphocytes, the cells that stimulate the body's immune response. Lymphosarcoma can affect the dog's lymph nodes, liver, spleen, and other organs, and it is most common in middle-aged or older dogs. Diagnosis is usually made after unidentified lumps or swellings are examined. If the cancer is found early enough, chemotherapy may add months or even years to the dog's life.

Osteosarcoma

Osteosarcoma is an aggressive cancer of the bone, and it is highly metastatic, meaning that it is prone to spreading to other parts of the body. Treatment usually involves amputation of the affected limb, followed by a course of chemotherapy. Success of treatment varies depending on how far the cancer has spread, but with proper treatment, some dogs live at least a year after treatment. A dog with osteosarcoma should in most cases be treated by a veterinary oncologist because of the aggressive nature of the disease and the rapid changes in cancer treatments.

Mammary Tumours

Mammary tumours may be small, benign growths in the breast tissue or large, aggressively metastatic cancers. This is the most common type of tumour in unspayed bitches (female dogs), and it usually appears when the bitch is between five and ten years old, although tumours sometimes affect younger bitches. This cancer is easily prevented—a bitch who is spayed before coming into her first heat has very little chance of developing mammary cancer. The risk is a bit higher if she's spayed after her first heat but before she's 2.5 years old and higher yet for bitches spayed later in life or never spayed. If they are detected early, mammary tumours in bitches can often be treated successfully, so if you feel any sort of growth in or around your

Is Your Dog Deaf?

Terriers are known to be independent minded, but that doesn't mean they shouldn't listen to you. If your dog seems to consistently not hear you, have him checked for deafness, an inherited problem affecting Parson and Jack Russell Terriers.

dog's teats, see your vet. Treatment may involve surgery, chemotherapy, and radiation therapy. Male dogs occasionally develop mammary tumours, and when they do, the tumours are usually aggressive and the prognosis is poor.

Testicular Tumours

Testicular tumours are among the most common tumours in older intact (unneutered) male dogs, and they are completely preventable by neutering. Testicular tumours are reasonably easy to diagnose, and surgical castration is usually all the treatment required, although more aggressive therapy may be needed in some cases. The risk of testicular cancer is much higher in dogs who have one or both testicles undescended into the scrotum, so the neutering of any dog with retained testicles is essential.

Ear Disorders

The following are ear disorders that are common in Parson and Jack Russell Terriers.

Deafness

One of the more serious inherited problems affecting Parson and Jack Russell Terriers is deafness. In very simple terms, inherited deafness in these breeds occurs when the gene for a white coat causes the pigment necessary for transmitting sound to be missing from certain organs in the ear. A dog with bilateral deafness is deaf in both ears and has no hearing whatsoever. A dog with unilateral deafness (sometimes called a "uni") is deaf in one ear.

It takes a very dedicated person with outstanding dog training skills and a safe environment to raise and train a totally deaf dog. Compassion is not enough; good intentions can lead to disaster if not supported by the skills, knowledge, and environment needed to manage a dog who can't hear. If you are up to the task, some excellent books and Internet resources do offer support and information for owners of deaf dogs.

A terrier with unilateral deafness can function normally as a pet, but owners need to be aware that the dog may have some relatively minor problems, such as initial difficulty locating the source of a sound. A bilaterally deaf dog is much more challenging, and because he hears nothing at all, requires an owner who is dedicated to keeping him safe and training him non-verbally.

No dog with any degree of deafness should ever be used for breeding. It's important to understand, too, that it's not always easy to determine deafness, especially unilateral deafness, because dogs respond to many stimuli, not just auditory stimuli. The Brainstem Auditory Evoked Response (BAER) test is used to determine partial or complete deafness in dogs. The test measures the brain's response to clicking sounds in each ear, and puppies can be tested any time after five weeks of age. Responsible breeders test all dogs prior to breeding them, and they test all puppies before they go to their new homes. Dogs who produce deaf puppies should not be used for further breeding.

Ear Infections

Otitis externa, or inflammation of the outer ear canal, is very common in dogs. Signs of infection or other problems in the ear include strong odour, rubbing or scratching of the ears and head, shaking or tilting the head, discharge from the ear, swelling or redness, and tenderness around the ears. To treat an ear infection effectively, accurate diagnosis is essential. If your terrier shows signs of ear problems, don't apply ear cleaners or medications without consulting your vet, as the wrong treatment can cause more damage and pain. To keep your dog's ears healthy, check them once a week and keep them clean. (For more information on how to do this, see Chapter 5.)

If your terrier is displaying signs of an ear infection, only apply ear cleaners or medications upon the advice of your vet.

Eye and Vision Problems

Parson and Jack Russell Terriers are potentially at risk for several eye disorders of varying severity. Unfortunately, many breeders still do not have their dogs screened for inherited eye disease, although more do every year. If you're buying a Parson or Jack Russell Terrier, your best bet for a puppy with healthy eyes is to buy from a breeder who breeds only dogs whose eyes have been cleared. Now, let's look at the eye problems known to exist in Russells.

Cataracts

A cataract is an opaque spot on the normally transparent lens of the eye. Cataracts, which may affect one or both eyes, may be visible to the naked eye as white or bluish dots on the eye's

surface. Juvenile cataracts are believed to be inherited, and affected dogs should not be used for breeding. Annual eye examinations are recommended for all breeding animals in order to detect juvenile cataracts early and to monitor any suspicious cataract to see if it progresses, or grows, which is typical of inherited cataracts.

Not all cataracts are inherited. They can also be caused by ageing (senile cataracts), environmental factors (like injury, exposure to dust, excessive heat, chemicals, radiation, and some medications), nutritional deficiencies, eye disease (persistent pupillary membrane [PPM] or progressive retinal atrophy [PRA]), or other diseases (diabetes, for example). If the cataract is so severe that the dog cannot see to get around, the lens can be surgically removed.

Distichiasis

Distichiasis is a condition involving abnormal growth of small hairs on the inner surfaces of the eyelids. The hairs irritate the cornea, causing inflammation of the affected eye, squinting, or frequent blinking, and in some cases a discharge from the eye. Distichiasis is treated by removing the hairs surgically or by electro-epilation, a process in which the hair and its root are destroyed by a small electrical charge. Infections caused by distichiasis are treated with antibiotic eye drops. If left untreated, distichiasis will become progressively worse, resulting in eye ulcers, infections, and blindness.

Glaucoma

Glaucoma is a serious condition in which abnormally high pressure in the eyeball prevents the proper supply of oxygen and nutrients to the cornea and lens and causes damage to the optic nerve. The usual result is partial or total blindness.

Primary glaucoma is inherited, while secondary glaucoma is caused by injury or disease. Early symptoms of glaucoma may include pain, and the dog may respond by rubbing his eye with his paw or against the floor or furniture, or by squinting or fluttering his eyelids. Other symptoms include a dilated pupil, cloudiness within the cornea, or enlarged blood vessels in the white of the eye. At first, only one eye is usually affected.

Immediate treatment—within hours—is essential. The pressure in the eye can quickly destroy cells in the retina and optic nerve and can damage the iris, the cornea, and the structures that hold

Causes of Ear Disorders

Ear disorders can be caused by the following factors:

- Allergies such as atopy or food allergies
- Parasites, like ear mites
- Microorganisms, like bacteria and yeast
- Foreign bodies, like plant awns
- Trauma
- Hormonal abnormalities
- Hereditary or immune conditions
- Tumours

the lens in position, and the dog will go blind. The eyeball itself will then swell, causing terrible pain. If caught early, the disease can sometimes be controlled, at least for a while, with eye drops and medication. Dogs with glaucoma should not be bred from.

Lens Luxation

Lens luxation occurs when the lens moves from its normal position behind the cornea. This disease appears in two forms: Secondary lens luxation results from injury to the eye and is not hereditary, while primary lens luxation is inherited, and dogs who are affected or who have produced affected puppies should not be used for breeding. It's a difficult problem for breeders to eliminate, though, because symptoms don't appear until the dog is three to eight years old, by which time he may already have been used for breeding.

Initially, only one eye will appear to be affected, but sooner (within weeks) or later (up to several years), symptoms will also appear in the other eye. The first signs of a problem may be behavioural changes due to changes in vision—the dog may bump into things or have trouble catching balls and biscuits. Untreated, lens luxation can cause glaucoma or corneal edema, diseases in which the normal flow of fluids through the cornea are restricted, causing pressure and pain in the eye. Eye drops and oral medications sometimes help, but in severe cases, it may be necessary to remove the lens or the entire eye.

It is easy to spot any abnormalities in the typically clear, alert, expressive eyes of a terrier.

Persistent Pupillary Membranes (PPMs)

Persistent pupillary membranes (PPMs) are the remnants of blood vessels that carry blood between parts of the eye during foetal development. These vessels normally resolve (disappear) shortly after the puppy is born. PPMs that link one part of the iris to another don't usually cause problems, but PPMs that link iris to cornea or iris to lens, or that occur massed in the anterior chamber of the eye, can cause severe vision problems or even blindness. There is no effective treatment for PPMs.

Progressive Retinal Atrophy (PRA)

Progressive Retinal Atrophy (PRA) (also known as Progressive Retinal Degeneration [PRD]) refers to a group of inherited diseases that cause blindness due to degeneration of vision cells in the retina. Early symptoms of PRA include loss of night vision, which will make the dog reluctant to go out at night or to negotiate stairs or furniture in darkened rooms. Eventually, he'll lose daylight vision as well. Cataracts sometimes occur eventually in dogs with PRA.

It is often necessary to have an affected dog re-examined several times at intervals to detect PRA, which is one reason that dogs used for breeding should have annual examinations by a veterinary ophthalmologist (your regular vet will not have the necessary equipment) and should not be bred if diagnosed with PRA. There is no treatment for progressive retinal atrophy.

Many responsible breeders have their terriers screened for inherited eye disease.

Heart and Blood Disorders

The following are some conditions of the heart and blood that are relatively common in Parson and Jack Russell Terriers.

Heart Disease

Heart disease can occur in Parson and Jack Russells, as in other dogs. One of the most common forms of canine heart disease is aortic stenosis (AS), which is a narrowing of the valve that passes blood from the left ventricle of the heart into the aorta, from which it flows to the rest of the body. The abnormally narrow opening causes the heart to work harder to force blood into the aorta, leading to hypertrophy (thickening) of the left heart muscle and dilation (ballooning) of the aorta due to the increased pressure. Because the flow of blood is reduced, many affected dogs faint or even die suddenly after exercising. A heart murmur may indicate aortic stenosis, but many murmurs do not.

Patent ductus arteriosus (PDA) occurs when the blood vessel that connects the aorta to the pulmonary artery in the foetus fails to close around the time of birth. Symptoms may include a heart murmur and exercise intolerance. In some cases, PDA can be corrected surgically.

If you're concerned that your terrier may have a heart disease, a veterinary cardiologist can perform an echocardiogram for a more accurate (although not foolproof) diagnosis. Weight control and restricted exercise can help lengthen the life of a dog with heart disease, and your vet may prescribe drugs to help improve heart function.

Von Willebrand's Disease

Von Willebrand's disease is an inherited bleeding disorder that occurs in many breeds. Typical symptoms of von Willebrand's in dogs include spontaneous bleeding from the nose or gums; blood in the urine or faeces; and excessive bleeding during surgery or after nail trimming. In an unspayed bitch, von Willebrand's may cause prolonged bleeding during oestrus or when delivering puppies, and a puppy with the disease can bleed to death when his umbilical cord is severed at birth. An affected dog may haemorrhage internally. Russells should be tested for von Willebrand's while they are young, in part because the disease can be harder to detect in older dogs, and in part to allow your vet to take precautions when performing surgery or other procedures with the potential to cause bleeding. Affected dogs should not be bred from.

Dogs suffering from von Willebrand's disease may experience spontaneous bleeding after a routine event like nail trimming.

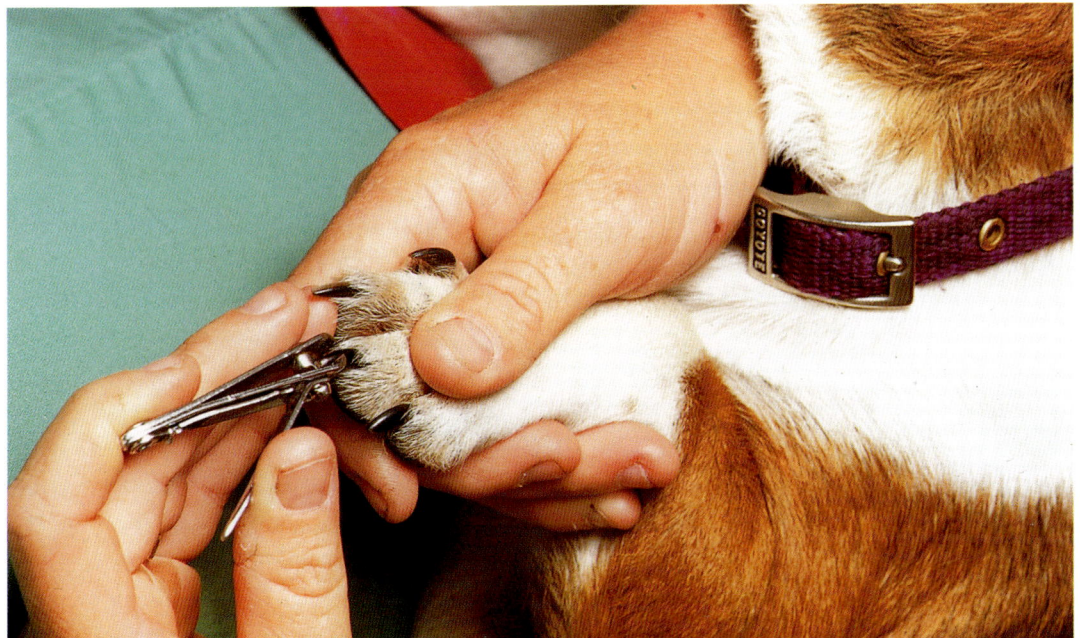

Orthopaedic Problems

Like many breeds of dogs, Parson and Jack Russell Terriers are susceptible to certain defects of the bones and joints.

Legg-Perthes Disease

Legg-Perthes disease (also called Legg-Calve-Perthes, or LCP) is a disease of the hip joint that occurs in several terrier breeds, including the Russells. The hip joint is essentially a ball-and-socket arrangement in which the head of the femur (the thigh bone) works as the "ball." In Legg-Perthes, the head of the femur slowly dies and disintegrates, causing the dog pain, arthritic changes, and lameness. Symptoms usually appear when the dog is 6 to 12 months old, and the disease is nearly always hereditary. Treatment for Legg-Perthes typically involves surgical removal of the head of the femur, after which the muscles compensate by forming a "false joint," enabling the dog to move freely again.

Patellar Luxation

Patellar luxation is a condition in which the patella (kneecap), located in the hind leg, luxates (slips) out of position. In a normal canine knee (or stifle), the patella slides along a groove in the femur (thighbone). If the groove is too shallow or otherwise malformed, the patella may slip. Sometimes it slips back into position, but often it remains out of position, locking the leg straight. Over time, the wear caused by this abnormal movement can cause painful arthritic changes. A luxating patella also predisposes the dog to torn cruciate ligaments and other injuries.

Some dogs suffer little if any disability from luxating patellas, and they need no treatment other than weight control and reasonable exercise. If an affected dog is consistently lame or suffers from other knee injuries, then surgical repair may be necessary to relieve pain and restore normal movement. While patellar luxation is not common in Russells, it does occur and is hereditary. Dogs with luxating patellas should not be bred from.

IN CASE OF EMERGENCY

As most of us know all too well, an emergency can happen in an instant. Smart as he is, your terrier can't assemble basic first-aid supplies and the critical information that might save his life in an emergency. You have to do it for him.

Canine First Aid

Being prepared for an emergency makes it much more likely that you'll be able to respond effectively. We don't have room here for more than the basics, so consider adding a good veterinary first-aid book to your home library, or take a pet first-aid or cardiopulmonary resuscitation (CPR) class, which may be offered by an education programme, veterinary school, or a veterinary practice. Then, if the unthinkable happens, give first-aid care and then call your vet to let her know you're coming.

Now let's look briefly at some common canine emergencies.

Poisoning

Our world is full of poisons, and no matter how careful we are, our dogs are sometimes exposed to them. Prescription and non-prescription medications can kill a dog, as can chocolate, raisins, or grapes. More than 700 types of plants, including many common house and garden plants, are toxic, as are fertilisers, herbicides, and insecticides. Pesticides, including slug bait, ant poisons, and mouse or rat poisons, are made to attract animals and are deadly. A terrier

First-Aid Kit for Dogs

Canine first-aid kits are available from many pet shops or vets, or you can assemble one yourself. Here's a list of basic supplies for a doggy first-aid kit:
- Muzzle to keep your dog from biting when in pain or frightened;
- Hydrogen peroxide in 3% solution (USP). Write the purchase date on the bottle, and replace annually with a fresh bottle;
- Bulb syringe or medicine syringe;
- Saline eye solution to flush eyes;
- Artificial tear gel to lubricate eyes after flushing;
- Anti-diarrhoeal (ask your vet's advice);
- Topical antibiotic;
- Mild grease-cutting dishwashing liquid to remove skin contaminants;
- Rubber gloves for handling contaminated dog;
- Forceps or tweezers;
- Good veterinary first-aid manual;
- Small notebook and pen or pencil for taking notes (for instance, time poison was ingested, time of a seizure, intervals between seizures, bowel movements, vomiting, etc.);
- Telephone numbers for your veterinary surgeon, who will provide emergency out-of-hours cover—and a friend or neighbour who could help in an emergency.

Weather Cautions

Never leave your dog in a vehicle on a warm day, even for a few minutes. Restrict his exercise in very hot weather, and don't leave him outside without shade or on concrete or asphalt. Cool, clean water should always be available, and if your dog has trouble breathing, a history of heatstroke, or is elderly or ill, keep him indoors and cool when the weather is hot.

can even be poisoned by eating a poisoned animal. Lead paint chips or dust, toys, curtain weights, fishing weights, lead shot, some tiles, some types of insulation, improperly glazed ceramic bowls, and water that's passed through lead pipes can all cause lead poisoning. Antifreeze is another poison that is sweet but lethal. Bees and wasps are a hazard in some parts of the country at certain times of the year. It's not surprising that many dogs are poisoned every year!

If you know or suspect that your dog has been exposed to poison, contact your veterinary surgeon immediately. Don't assume that your dog is safe if you don't see symptoms—some poisons do much of their damage before symptoms appear, and waiting to start treatment could make the difference between life and death. Symptoms of poisoning may include some or all of the following: vomiting; diarrhoea; loss of appetite; swelling of the tongue and other mouth tissues, face, or body; excessive salivation; staggering; seizures; and collapse.

Fractures

Fractures, or broken bones, are not uncommon in active dogs. If you think your dog has fractured a bone, keep him quiet to prevent more damage to the bone or surrounding tissue, nerves, and blood vessels. Fractures of bones in the head, neck, and body can be life threatening, so it's vital to prevent movement. Don't assume that if your dog can walk, his leg isn't broken.

Don't try to apply a splint unless you've had first-aid training, because you could cause more damage. Keep the dog quiet, carry him on a blanket or board to a vehicle, and get him to your veterinary surgeon without delay.

How a fracture is treated will depend on its location and severity and the dog's age, but veterinary care is essential for all fractures, to control pain and prevent more damage.

Cuts and Bites

An active terrier is also likely to suffer cuts or bites and bleeding sometime in his life. In this case, begin by evaluating the injury. The amount of bleeding isn't necessarily an indication of how serious the wound is; some areas, such as the nose and tongue, bleed profusely even from tiny cuts, while some serious injuries barely bleed at all. If the injury is minor, clean it gently with hydrogen

peroxide, and apply pressure with a clean towel or gauze pad until the bleeding stops. Then, apply a topical antibiotic ointment and watch the area for a few days for signs of infection. If the wound is bleeding heavily and is deep or long, apply pressure with a clean towel, cloth, or gauze pad, and get your dog to your vet as soon as possible. He may need stitches and other treatment.

Restrict your Russell's outdoor activities on very hot days to prevent heatstroke.

Bite wounds are always at a high risk of infection because of large populations of bacteria in the mouth. Bites may also introduce disease. If your dog is bitten by another animal, clean the wound and call your vet. Many bites do not bleed, which may seem like a good thing, but punctures that don't bleed trap bacteria and can develop serious infections. Even if the wound itself doesn't require veterinary care, your vet will probably prescribe an oral antibiotic.

Heatstroke

Dogs don't sweat, and they can't cool themselves as efficiently as we do, making them prone to heatstroke (hyperthermia), a life-threatening condition that occurs when an animal's body temperature rises beyond a safe level. Symptoms of heatstroke include red or pale gums; bright-red tongue; sticky, thick saliva; rapid panting; and vomiting and/or diarrhoea. The dog may act dizzy or weak, and he may go into shock.

A dog with moderate heatstroke (body temperature from 104° to 106°F [40° to 41.1°C]) will probably recover if given immediate first aid. Use a hose, shower, or bath of cool, but not cold, water to wet and cool him, and check his temperature every ten minutes. When it's down to 103°F (39.4°C), give him a rehydration fluid or water and get him to a vet.

Severe heatstroke (body temperature over 106°F [41.1°C]) can kill your dog or cause permanent damage to internal organs. If you're more than five minutes from the vet and your dog is conscious, follow the cooling procedures outlined above until his temperature is down to 106°F (41.1°C). Then, loosely wrap him in a lightweight, cool wet towel or blanket and get him to a vet without delay.

The vet will continue to monitor your dog's temperature and continue the cooling process if necessary. She will check for shock, breathing problems, kidney failure, and other potential complications, and she will administer fluids. Once a dog has had heatstroke, he's more susceptible to a recurrence, so be especially careful not to put him in risky situations, and ask your vet about follow-up care.

Frostbite is not common in dogs, but it can affect your pet if he is out in very cold weather for too long.

Frostbite

Frostbite, the formation of ice crystals in body tissues, is not common in dogs, but it can affect your dog if he's out in severely cold weather for too long. The ice crystals restrict the flow of blood in the injured area, and if not treated, gangrene (tissue death) can occur. Frostbite is often hard to detect on a dog, but signs include redness of the skin initially with a shift to white or grey, most commonly in the ear tips, toes, and tail.

The first thing to do if you suspect your dog is frostbitten is to get him to a warmer place. Then, apply warm (about 102°F) compresses to the affected areas, or immerse the area in warm water. When the area feels warm, gently pat—don't rub—it dry. Keep your dog warm, and get him to a vet immediately.

ALTERNATIVE APPROACHES TO

Normal Vital Signs

- A dog's normal temperature is 99.5 to 102.8°F (37.5 to 39.3°C).
- A dog's normal heart rate is 60 to 120 beats per minute.
- A dog normally takes 14 to 22 breaths per minute.

CANINE HEALTH CARE

Many pet owners have become interested in non-traditional approaches to animal as well as human health over the past few decades. The terms alternative, complementary, or holistic medicine are often used to refer to formal disciplines such as chiropractic, acupuncture, homeopathy, herbal therapy, and nutrition, and to other practices such as massage therapy, shiatsu, reiki, TTouch, Contact Reflex, and others. The belief that physical and emotional factors work together to create health or illness is the common thread tying all of these approaches to wellness together.

Homeopathy

Homeopathic medicine treats symptoms of illness with minute, diluted amounts of substances that, in larger doses, would cause those same symptoms. The goal is to stimulate the body to respond by curing itself. Most homeopathic substances come from plants, although some are from animal and mineral sources. Homeopathic treatments are said by some people to be effective in treating diseases, allergies, injuries, and poisons, but some of the substances used can be toxic in the wrong doses. As a result, it's not a good idea to try homeopathic remedies without consulting a veterinary surgeon who is trained in homeopathic veterinary medicine.

Acupuncture

Acupuncture was developed in ancient China. In modern veterinary usage, needles, massage, heat, and lasers are used to stimulate the release of hormones, endorphin, and other chemical substances that enable the body to fight off pain and disease.

Chiropractic

Chiropractic medicine deals with the relationship between the spinal column and the nervous system, and its effect on overall

What to Do if Your Dog Is Lost

Despite your best precautions, your dog could become lost sometime in his life. The following steps can increase your chances of bringing him home safe and sound.

- Identification—Attach a name tag to your dog's collar so that anyone who finds him can also find you. Make sure the information is current. Collars and tags can get lost or be removed, so consider having your dog tattooed or microchipped for permanent identification. These measures, in addition to a good photograph of your dog, also give you proof of ownership if that is ever disputed.
- Act fast—The sooner you begin a serious search, the better the chances that you'll find your dog.
- Advertise—Advertise in your local newspaper, and consider running ads in newspapers from neighbouring towns as well—a dog can travel a long way in a short time.
- Call—Call all rescue centres, terrier rescue organisations, and vets in your area. Visit rescue centres frequently to check for yourself; staff could overlook your dog or fail to recognise him as a Parson or Jack Russell Terrier.
- Use the Internet—Use the Internet to post information about your dog to discussion lists and bulletin boards, and ask that the information be forwarded to other appropriate lists.
- Post flyers—Post flyers with a colour photo of your dog with information on where and when he was lost, and your telephone number.
  - Ask neighbourhood children—Neighbourhood children are more likely than adults to know what's going on at "street level." Ask area schools for permission to hang your poster where pupils will see it.

The faster you respond if your dog is lost, the better your chances of finding him.

health. Many competitors find that regular chiropractic adjustments improve their dogs' performances.

Herbal Therapy

Herbal therapy can be highly effective, but herbs should be used with great caution and only under the supervision of someone who is knowledgeable about their properties. Some herbs are highly toxic.

YOUR AGEING TERRIER

The age at which any individual dog becomes "elderly" varies, but you can expect to start seeing age-related changes when your terrier is between 9 and 12 years old. First, he'll probably begin to slow down a bit. He may become more attached to his daily routine and less tolerant of changes. You may notice some changes in his hearing and vision, and his body may feel "bony" as he loses muscle tone and weight. He may also move more slowly and appear stiff.

Many elderly dogs also exhibit behavioural changes. Your elderly terrier may seem anxious about things he hardly noticed before. He may be confused by changes in his environment or routine, or he may become anxious when you're away from him. He'll probably become less active, and he may sleep more.

Your elderly dog may not solicit your attention as often as he used to, but never forget that he still loves you and needs your attention and affection. Snuggles and belly rubs are as important as ever to your dog's emotional well-being. Older dogs can become lonely and depressed, so be sure to give him some special time every day.

Regular, gentle grooming also remains important. Brushing will help keep his muscles and joints supple and will stimulate his circulation. Grooming will also alert you to lumps and bumps that need veterinary attention. Your older dog should continue to get moderate exercise to promote physical and mental health.

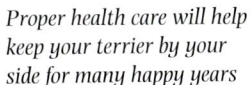

Proper health care will help keep your terrier by your side for many happy years

Gradual changes are a normal part of the ageing process, but if you notice a sudden or extreme change in your dog's body or behaviour, take him to your vet. Even if he's in good health, be sure that your old friend gets regular check-ups at least annually. Many vets recommend examinations every six months for their older dogs.

Most of us know better than to take good health for granted, whether our own or that of our doggy friends. Even if your terrier seems to be healthy, he should have regular veterinary check-ups and preventive care, receive sufficient exercise, and eat a healthy diet. Proper care will help keep your terrier by your side for many happy years to come.

THE KENNEL CLUB BREED STANDARD
(PARSON RUSSELL TERRIER)

General Appearance: Workmanlike, active and agile; built for speed and endurance. Overall picture of balance and flexibility. Honourable scars permissible.

Characteristics: Essentially a working terrier with ability and conformation to go to ground and run with hounds.

Temperament: Bold and friendly.

Head and Skull: Flat, moderately broad, gradually narrowing to the eyes. Shallow stop. Length from nose to stop slightly shorter than from stop to occiput. Nose black.

Eyes: Almond-shaped, fairly deep-set, dark, keen expression.

Ears: Small, V-shaped, dropping forward, carried close to head, tip of ear to reach corner of eye, fold not to appear above top of skull. Leather of moderate thickness.

Mouth: Jaws strong, muscular. Teeth with a perfect, regular and complete scissor bite, i.e. upper teeth closely overlapping lower teeth and set square to the jaws.

Neck: Clean, muscular, of good length, gradually widening to shoulders.

Forequarters: Shoulders long and sloping, well laid back, cleanly cut at withers. Legs strong, must be straight with joints turning neither in nor out. Elbows close to body, working free of the sides.

Body: Ribs not over-sprung. Chest of moderate depth, not to come below point of elbow, capable of being spanned behind the shoulders by average size hands. Back strong and straight. Loin slightly arched. Well balanced. Overall length slightly longer than height from withers to ground.

Hindquarters: Strong, muscular with good angulation and bend of stifle. Hocks set low and rear pasterns parallel giving plenty of drive.

Feet: Compact with firm pads, turning neither in nor out.

Tail: Customarily docked. *Docked:* Length complimenting the body while providing a good handhold. Strong, straight, moderately high set, carried well up on the move. *Undocked:* Of moderate length and as straight as possible, giving a general balance to the dog, thick at the root and tapering towards the end. Moderately high set, carried well up on the move.

Gait/Movement: Free-striding, well co-ordinated; straight action front and behind.

Coat: Naturally harsh, close and dense, whether rough or smooth. Belly and undersides coated. Skin must be thick and loose.

Colour: Entirely white or predominantly white with tan, lemon or black markings, or any combination of these colours, preferably confined to the head and/or root of tail.

Size: Most importantly a working terrier should be capable of being spanned behind the shoulders by average sized hands. Ideal height at withers: dogs 36 cms (14 ins.), bitches 33 cms (13 ins.) It is recognised that smaller terriers are required for work in certain areas and lower heights are therefore quite acceptable provided that soundness and balance are maintained.

Faults: Any departure from the foregoing points should be considered a fault and the seriousness with which the fault should be regarded should be in exact proportion to its degree and its effect upon the health and welfare of the dog.

General Appearance: Male animals should have two apparently normal testicles fully descended into the scrotum.

© The Kennel Club
Reproduced with their permission *Last Updated - November 2002*

THE JACK RUSSELL TERRIER CLUB OF GREAT BRITAIN BREED STANDARD

Characteristics: The terrier must present a lively, active and alert appearance. It should impress with its fearless and happy disposition. It should be remembered that the Jack Russell is a working terrier and should retain these instincts. Nervousness, cowardice and over-aggression should be discouraged, and it should always appear confident.

General Appearance: A sturdy, tough terrier, very much on its toes all the time, measuring between 10" and 15" at the withers. The body length must be in proportion to the height, and it should present a compact, balanced image, always being in solid, hard condition.

Head: Should be well balanced and in proportion to the body. The skull should be flat, of moderate width at the ears, narrowing to the eyes. There should be a defined stop but not over-pronounced. The length of muzzle from the nose to the stop should be slightly shorter than the distance from the stop to the occiput. The nose should be black. The jaw should be powerful and well boned with strongly muscled cheeks.

Eyes: Should be almond shaped, dark in colour and full of life and intelligence.

Ears: Small "V" shaped drop ears carried forward close to the head and of moderate thickness.

Mouth: Strong teeth with the top slightly overlapping the lower.

Neck: Clean and muscular, of good length, gradually widening at the shoulders.

Forequarters: The shoulders should be sloping and well laid back, fine at points and clearly cut at the withers. Forelegs should be strong and straight boned with joints in correct alignment. Elbows hanging perpendicular to the body and working free of the sides.

Body: The chest should be shallow, narrow and the front legs set not too widely apart, giving an athletic, rather than heavily chested appearance. As a guide only, the chest should be small enough to be easily spanned behind the shoulders, by average hands, when the terrier is in a fit, working condition. The back should be strong, straight and, in comparison to the height of the terrier, give a balanced image. The loin should be slightly arched.

Hindquarters: Should be strong and muscular, well put together with good angulations and hand of stifle, giving plenty of drive and propulsion. Looking from behind, the hocks must be straight.

Feet: Round, hard-padded, of cat-like appearance, neither turning in nor out.

Tail: Should be set rather high, carried gaily and in proportion to body length, usually about four inches long, providing a good hand-hold.

Coat: Smooth, without being so sparse as not to provide a certain amount of protection from the elements and undergrowth. Rough or broken coated, without being woolly.

Colour: White should predominate with tan, black, or brown markings. Brindle markings are unacceptable.

Gait: Movement should be free, lively, well co-ordinated with straight action in front and behind.

Notes: (1) Dogs and bitches should be entire and capable of breeding. Dogs should be shown to have both testicles fully descended into the scrotum. (2) Old scars or injuries, the result of work or accident, should not be allowed to prejudice the terrier's chance in the show ring unless they interfere with its movement or with its utility for work or stud. (3) For showing purposes, terriers are classified into two groups according to their height, which are 10 to 12.5 ins and over 12.5 to 15 ins.

The Jack Russell Terrier of Great Britain Breed Standard was the first breed standard for a Jack Russell Terrier to be drawn up.

BREED CLUBS AND KENNEL CLUBS

American Kennel Club (AKC)
5580 Centerview Drive,
Raleigh, NC 27606
Telephone: 919 233 9767
Fax: 919 233 3627
E-mail: info@akc.org
www.akc.org

Canadian Kennel Club (CKC)
89 Skyway Avenue, Suite 100
Etobicoke, Ontario M9W 6R4
Telephone: 416 675 5511
Fax: 416 675 6506
E-mail: information@ckc.ca
www.ckc.ca

Federation Cynologique Internationale (FCI)
Secretariat General de la FCI
Place Albert 1er, 13B – 6530 Thuin
Belqique
www.fci.be

Jack Russell Terrier Club of America
P.O. Box 4527
Lutherville, MD 21094-4527
Telephone: (410) 561-3655
Fax: (410) 560-2563
E-mail: JRTCA@worldnet.att.net
www.jrtca.com

Jack Russell Terrier Cub of Great Britain
General enquiries: Adrian Guthrie.
E-mail: jrtcbgnatsec@hotmail.co.uk
http://www.jackrussellgb.co.uk

Parson Jack Russell Terrier Club
Secretary: Mrs R. M. Jussey Wilford.
Telephone: 01905 821440

Parson Russell Terrier Association of America (PRTAA)
P.O. Box 199
North Hatfield, MA 01066
E-mail: klbaker1@verizon.net
www.prtaa.org

The Kennel Club
1 Clarges Street
London
W1J 8AB
Telephone: 0870 606 6750
Fax: 0207 518 1058
www.the-kennel-club.org.uk

United Kennel Club (UKC)
100 E. Kilgore Road
Kalamazoo, MI 49002-5584
Telephone: 269 343 9020
Fax: 269 343 7037
E-mail: pbickell@ukcdogs.com
www.ukcdogs.com

PET SITTERS

National Association of Registered Petsitters
www.dogsit.com

UK Petsitters
Telephone: 01902 41789
www.ukpetsitter.com

Dog Services UK
www.dogservices.co.uk

RESCUE ORGANISATIONS AND ANIMAL WELFARE GROUPS

British Veterinary Association Animal Welfare Foundation (BVA AWF)
7 Mansfield Street
London W1G 9NQ
Telephone: 0207 636 6541
Fax: 0207 436 2970

Email: bva-awf@bva.co.uk
www.bva-awf.org.uk/about

Parson Russell Terrier Welfare
General enquiries: Caroline Ross
Telephone: 01775 840391
E-mail: tiggertooprt@aol.com

Royal Society for the Prevention of Cruelty to Animals (RSPCA)
Telephone: 0870 3335 999
Fax: 0870 7530 284
www.rspca.org.uk

Scottish Society for the Prevention of Cruelty to Animals (SSPCA)
Braehead Mains, 603 Queensferry Road
Edinburgh EH4 6EA
Telephone: 0131 339 0222
Fax: 0131 339 4777
Email: enquiries@scottishspca.org
www.scottishspca.org/about

SPORTS

Agility Club UK
www.agilityclub.co.uk

British Flyball Association
PO Box 109, Petersfield GU32 1XZ
Telephone: 01753 620110
Fax: 01726 861079
Email: bfa@flyball.org.uk
www.flyball.org.uk

Canine Freestyle Federation, Inc.
Secretary: Brandy Clymire
E-Mail: secretary@canine-freestyle.org
www.canine-freestyle.org

International Agility Link (IAL)
Global Administrator: Steve Drinkwater
E-mail: yunde@powerup.au
www.agilityclick.com/~ial

World Canine Freestyle Organisation
P.O. Box 350122Brooklyn, NY 11235-2525
Telephone: (718) 332-8336
www.worldcaninefreestyle.org

THERAPY

Pets As Therapy
3 Grange Farm Cottages
Wycombe Road, Saunderton
Princes Risborough
Bucks HP27 9NS
Telephone: 0870 977 0003
Fax: 0870 706 2562
www.petsastherapy.org

Therapy Dogs International (TDI)
88 Bartley Road
Flanders, NJ 07836
Telephone: (973) 252-9800
Fax: (973) 252-7171
E-mail: tdi@gti.netwww.tdi-dog.org

TRAINING AND BEHAVIOUR

Association of Pet Dog Trainers (APDT)
PO Box 17
Kempsford GL7 4W7
Telephone: 01285 810811

Association of Pet Behaviour Counsellors
PO Box 46
Worcester WR8 9YS
Telephone: 01386 751151
Fax: 01386 750743
Email: info@apbc.org.uk
www.apbc.org.uk

VETERINARY AND HEALTH RESOURCES

Association of British Veterinary Acupuncturists (ABVA)
66A Easthorpe, Southwell
Nottinghamshire NG25 0HZ
Email: jonnyboyvet@hotmail.com
www.abva.co.uk

Association of Chartered Physiotherapists Specialising in Animal Therapy (ACPAT)
52 Littleham Road
Exmoouth, Devon EX8 2QJ
Telephone/Fax: 01395 270648
Email: bexsharples@hotmail.com
www.acpat.org.uk

British Association of Homoeopathic Veterinary Surgeons
Alternative Veterinary
Medicine Centre
Chinham House
Stanford in the Vale
Oxfordshire SN7 8NQ
Email: enquiries@bahvs.com
www.bahvs.com

British Association of Veterinary Opthalmologists (BAVO)
Email: hjf@vetspecialists.co.uk
Email: secretary@bravo.org.uk
www.bravo.oprg.uk

British Small Animal Veterinary Association (BSAVA)
Woodrow House, 1 Telford Way
Waterwells Business Park
Quedgley, Gloucester GL2 2AB
Telephone: 01452 726700
Fax: 01452 726701
Email: customerservices@bsava.com
www.bsava.com

British Veterinary Association (BVA)
7 Mansfield Street, LondonW1G 9NQ
Telephone: 020 7636 6541
Fax: 020 7436 2970
E-mail: bvahq@bva.co.uk
www.bva.co.uk

British Veterinary Hospitals Association (BHVA)
Station Bungalow
Main Road, Stockfield
Northumberland NE43 7HJ
Telephone: 07966 901619
Fax: 07813 915954
Email: office@bvha.org.uk
www.BVHA.org.uk

Royal College of Veterinary Surgeons (RCVS)
Belgravia House, 62-64 Horseferry Road, London SW1P 2AF
Telephone: 0207 222 2001
Fax: 0207 222 2004
Email: admin@rcvs.org.uk
www.rcvs.org.uk

NEWSPAPERS AND MAGAZINES

Dog World Ltd
Somerfield House
Wotton Road, Ashford
Kent TN23 6LW
Telephone: 01233 621877
Fax: 01233 645669

Dogs Monthly
Ascot House, High Street,
Ascot, Berkshire SL5 7JG
Telephone: 0870 730 8433
Fax: 0870 730 8431
E-mail: admin@rtc-associates.freeserve.co.uk
www.corsini.co.uk/dogsmonthly

Dogs Today
Town Mill, Bagshot Road
Chobham, Surrey GU24 8BZ
Telephone: 01276 858880
Fax: 01276 858860
Email:
enquiries@dogstodaymagazine.co.uk
www.dogstodaymagazine.co.uk

Kennel Gazette
Kennel Club
1 Clarges Street
London W1J 8AB
Telephone: 0870 606 6750
Fax: 0207 518 1058
www.the-kennel-club.co.uk

K9 Magazine
21 High Street
Warsop
Nottinghamshire NG20 0AA
Telephone: 0870 011 4114
Fax: 0870 706 4564
Email: mail@k9magazine.com
www.k9magazine.com

Our Dogs
Our Dogs Publishing
5 Oxford Road
Station Approach
Manchester M60 1SX
www.ourdogs.co.uk

Your Dog
Roebuck House
33 Broad Street
Stamford
Lincolnshire PE9 1RB
Telephone: 01780 766199
Fax: 01780 766416

BOOKS

Barnes, Julia
Living With a Rescued Dog
Dorking: Interpet Publishing, 2004

Evans, J M & White, Kay
Doglopaedia
Dorking: Ringpress, 1998

Evans, J M
Book of The Bitch
Dorking: Ringpress, 1998

Tennant, Colin
*Mini Encyclopedia of Dog Training &
Behaviour*
Dorking: Interpet Publishing, **2005**

Evans, J M
What If my Dog?
Dorking: Interpet Publishing, **2006**

WEBSITES

Responsible Dog Breeding
www.britishdogbreeders.co.uk
A cornucopia of information and
pertinent links on responsible dog
breeding for British breeders.

Dog Behaviour
www.dogbehaviour.com
Canine Behaviourist Gwen Bailey's site,
filled with useful advice on canine
behaviour, communication, and
relevant links.

Petfinder
http://www.pet-locator.co.uk/
Search shelters and rescue groups for
adoptable pets.

ABOUT THE AUTHOR

Sheila Webster Boneham, Ph.D., loves dogs and writing about dogs. Three of her books have won the prestigious Maxwell Award from the Dog Writers Association of America, including *The Simple Guide to Labrador Retrievers,* named Best Single Breed Book of 2002. For the past decade, Sheila has taught people about dogs through her writing and other activities. She hopes that her successes and mistakes as a puppy buyer, breeder, trainer, owner, and rescuer can benefit other dog lovers and their dogs. Sheila and her canine companions are active in competition and in dog-assisted activities and therapy. A former university writing teacher, Sheila also conducts writing workshops. You can visit Sheila and her dogs on the web at www.sheilaboneham.com.

PHOTO CREDITS

Photo on page 51 courtesy of Mary Bloom.
Photos on pages 16, 45, 60, and 84 courtesy of Paulette Braun.
Photo on page 193 courtesy of Judith E. Strom.
All other photos courtesy of Isabelle Francais and T.F.H. archives.